LETTERS TO ELIZA

I left your mother, I didn't leave you

Kimberley Alice

Self Published

DEDICATION

*I dedicate this book to my daughter
Eliza, even though we are separated by
hatred and spitefulness I love you with
all my heart and I always will, forever,
hoping that love will win the day.*

ACKNOWLEDGMENTS

I thank my wife for being my rock, without your support this book would never have been written, your patience and understanding combined with your attention to detail and commitment to ensure that my side of the story has been portrayed so accurately is just amazing, thank you, this book has provided me with a way to release the pain I had held onto for so long and to finally move forward with my life in such a positive way at long last.

I would like to thank my family and friends for supporting me through what can only be described as a dark point in my life, a time that has been made so much brighter with their patience and understanding and much needed ongoing support, you have all provided me with the lifeline I needed to keep going and to emerge out the other side even stronger.

CHAPTER ONE

Burgers and Chaos

The Beginning of the End T-Minus 28 months before your due date of September 7, 2022.

May 30, 2020, at 21.04hrs

Dear Eliza,

This started two years before you were born, your mother kicked me out of the flat AGAIN. She messaged me saying don't bother coming home tonight and that she is going to throw all my stuff outside in the front garden at 08.00am tomorrow morning. She messaged me saying don't be late collecting my stuff off the floor tomorrow morning, because people will steal all my belongings. She knows that when she speaks to me like this it raises my anxiety levels and makes me panic with fear, but she is angry yet again with me over something so small and trivial, but your mother is the queen of overreacting and blowing minor things out of proportion.

I am at a friend's house they are cooking up some food in their garden on their bar-b-q and they asked me if I was hungry, I had been working on my bike all day, so I popped in to grab myself a burger, your mother knew I was there, because my friends had tagged me in a post on social media holding a big fat burger in my hand, your mother saw me eating this burger with my friends and she instantly became jealous because she wasn't there with me, this is what your mother does to me if she knows I am round someone's house, It doesn't matter who's house it is, it could be my parents' house or one of my friends' houses, your mother starts messaging me threatening me, terrorizing my head holding all my thoughts to ransom, emotionally blackmailing me into doing what she wants me to do, your mother plays the most horrendous mind games with me, bullying me into returning back to her at the flat, just so I am right under her nose, I am not

2

allowed to have fun without her being there, she has to be able to see and hear everything I do and say to people, your mother is insecure and paranoid and the most awful dominating control freak and she is ruining my life.

As usual, I try to message back and reason with her, she knows I will do this, she knows I will spend my time trying to reason with her, it gives her the attention she is craving through her insecurities, she loves the drama of making me feel unhappy whilst feeding into her insatiable need for attention and to boost her fragile ego, I have learnt over the last four years that I have no control over anything your mother says or does, I have watched her patterns of abuse towards me forming, I can predict her behavior now, I have come to accept that I have no control over what she does and says at all, and have learnt all I can do it stay out of her way while she is raging, so I just try to put some safe distance between us until she calms down and right now standing in my friends back garden eating a juicy burger is the safest place I know of, so I am not budging from this spot.

Your mother is trying to make me go back to her at the flat because she is sat all by herself alone and I am out having fun with friends, your mother is using emotional blackmail tactics to get me to return back to her, and because I am not doing what she wants me to do, her messages and her threats are increasing, I cannot explain this behavior to other people for they just would not believe the insane things I am saying to describe how our relationship has become, I have kept all of what has been going on between us private and to myself, I have never told anyone of your mothers behavior, until now! As I began to receive your mothers' abusive vile messages I decided to show my friend, I handed my phone over to him for him to read her messages for himself and the look on his face confirmed what I had been thinking for a while now, that your mother is abusive and the whole situation between us is just not right, and it is not healthy.

My friend advised me to turn my phone off so I couldn't see any of the messages being delivered, he advised me to ignore your mother and to not go rushing off back to her, my friend could see that your mother had learnt to control me through fear, that she was sending messages that were playing with my emotions and my fear responses. He explained that this tactic would only ever get worse and that if I didn't start standing up for myself that I was heading for a mental breakdown, he put his arm around my shoulders at this point as he could see I was about to break down right in front of him and cry!

Here starts the social stigma.............. men can't cry! I couldn't allow myself to cry in front of my male friend, I was a man, and men don't cry in front of other people and especially in front of other men!

We had all been friends for years, we were all at school together and had remained friends ever since, I was struggling to hold my shit together when his wife came over and read the foul messages, the happy look on her face changed to one of utter terror and concern for me, my friends have been concerned for me for some time now, they had seen some drastic changes in me, they had all noticed that in the last four years since being with your mother that I had lost weight, become quieter and more withdrawn, they also noticed that every time they had invited me to go out with them I was always declining their invitations, in all honesty I am embarrassed to go out, as I know your mother would have to come with me and her behavior is embarrassing for me, she is loud and rude to people, she has no filter and says the most upsetting things to people and I find myself making excuses or apologizing for her, I just don't want to do that anymore.

It is not my responsibility to apologize for your mother, she is an adult and capable of apologizing for herself, she has this arrogant mindset that she can't do anything wrong and everyone else is the one with the problem, it is never her fault, other people made her act like that, or made her say the awful things she says, I came to realize that I could no longer defend this toxic attitude of hers. I think this was the day that I reached the point of no return for me, my eyes were truly open to the sinister insidious nature of your mother and I no longer wanted to be terrorized by her.

I wanted to stay with my friends, they were happy, I felt comfortable in their company, I felt safe standing there in their back garden with my burger in my hand, I hadn't eaten all day, and I was hungry. I found that I was regularly skipping meals, and I was always trying to find reasons to stay out of the flat so I didn't have to go back to your mother, her company had become toxic, and her constant drama sagas and bad behavior was beginning to drain the life out of me, I couldn't cope with it anymore, I could feel myself breaking.

The sad thing is, it wasn't always like this, the first few years with your mother were happier, she seemed happier in herself, but then over time she reached a point where nothing I did made her happy, everything I did caused her to become angry and rude towards me, she constantly picked fault in everything I did, she belittled me, she ridiculed me, she would laugh at me and make me feel sad and upset. Your mother seemed to gain some kind of sick pleasure in hurting me and instead of walking away at this point, I found myself working even harder at trying to do things the way your mother wanted me to do them, but even trying harder and working harder didn't make your mother happy.

But instead of leaving, I stayed!

I held onto the hope that our relationship would become happier again, that your mother would suddenly change back into the happier person she was when we first got together, I held onto this hope for a further two years, she never changed at all over the next two years, she remained the same and my hope of happiness with her began to fade.

When we first got together your mother gave off the impression that she was a very confident capable women, but this was a lie, she projected this false image of her being this confident person when she was in fact extremely jealous and insecure. Your mother began accusing me of talking to other women, she had hacked my social media accounts and had looked through all my friends lists, she had made a note of all the females on my account and had stalked them all, your mother had made several fake social media accounts and had used these to spy on the women I knew.

Your mother became jealous and aggressive if I left the flat without her, she would constantly phone me and message me the whole time I was away from her she constantly accused of seeing other women and having exe girlfriends on my social media. I would return home to accusations of talking to women behind your mothers back or seeing other women, these false accusations would cause many rows and arguments that could go on for weeks, the moment I left the house every morning to go to work your mother would start messaging me, and this would go on all day, your mother would become angry and abusive if I didn't reply back to her relentless messages within seconds, leading to further accusations of me being with another woman, your mother would start throwing in women's names accusing me of being round their house, she would demand to know everything about the women on my social media, she wanted to know how I knew them and when was the last time I spoke to them.

Your mother started going through my phone to see who had called me that day and who had messaged me. I found myself deleting all this information before I returned home every day, which actually added to your mothers' accusations of me hiding things, but I just couldn't handle the arguments it was causing, I also deleted calls and messages off my phone to protect the people who were contacting me, as I knew your mother would target them and harass them, she would make a note of their names and take down their mobile numbers and call them or message them, your mother would look these people up on social media using her fake profiles and stalk their accounts, this was embarrassing for me.

I started to receive messages from friends and family saying they had been contacted by someone by the name of Julie or some other random name, asking personal questions about who they were and how they knew me, I had to explain that is was most likely to be your mother and I had to explain why she was contacting them and asking such questions, I had to explain that it was nothing they had done wrong at all, and that is was your mothers jealousy causing her to do the things she was doing, needless to say I lost a lot of friends this way, they all started to remove themselves off my social media accounts, another way of your mother isolating me away from the people that meant a lot to me.

> *I knew that this behavior was not healthy,*
> *but I just didn't know how to stop it.*

The next two years I lived my life in constant fear of what your mother was going to do or say to other people, I was in a constant state of anxiety never knowing what dramas your mother was going to cause for me, this had become a daily occurrence now, repeated toxic behavior that I was left to try to calm down the anger and aggression directed towards me, I had become your mothers emotional punch bag, constantly accused of lying and cheating on her, she pushed me to breaking point, but I still stayed with her, I lived in hope of changing her view of me, I thought that she would eventually see that I was not lying to her or cheating, your mothers previous partner, your brothers father had cheated on your mother, and I felt she was punishing me for the hurt he had caused your mother, she made me feel like she hated men and hated being with me, I really don't understand why she was with me, after all the horrible things she said to me, how I was not worthy of love or happiness, she told me what a horrible person I was and how stupid I was she was always putting me down, I began to question my own sense of self and my self-worth had plummeted since I had started dating your mother, I questioned every single little thing now, I used to be so much more confident, I never used to over think things like I do now. I felt like I was not even a person anymore and I could feel myself unravelling.

My tactic has always been to sit tight and wait until your mothers' rage subsided, this could go on for days, and sometimes for weeks, I just never knew how long I would be punished for, my life now consisted of treading on eggshells working so hard not to upset your mother, but I really don't know how much longer I can go on like this for. I've been desperately waiting for things to change.

All my love

Dad

CHAPTER TWO

So, that's it then?

Collection of my stuff from your mothers flat T-Minus 28 months before your due date.

May 31, 2020

Dear Eliza,

Following on from last night's hateful rage attack by your mother, I collected all my belongings from the flat and moved out; after confiding in my friends I decided last night that I could no longer endure being threatened and mentally coerced and manipulated into doing all the things your mother wanted me to do.

No matter what I did or how I did it, despite being screamed at by your mother with precise directions as to how, when and why she wanted me to do certain things, I always found I was still in the wrong anyway, I decided that last night's drama by your mother was enough to make me leave, I just wanted to be allowed to live my life my way, I wanted to be in control of myself, I had no respite from your mothers commands, she just never let up at all.

When I collected all my things from the flat and moved out leaving the front door key on the side your mother was in shock, she was shocked that I actually moved all my things out and walked away, she told me that she never thought I would leave her, even after the horrendous treatment by her, she told me she never thought I would actually have the courage to leave her.

I was taken aback by this, your mother knew damn well that I was terrified of her, she counted on me being too scared to leave her, she thought I would never leave and that she was free to continue to treat me so badly without me putting up any kind of resistance to her, she had broken me down over time and now her telling me she thought this toxic situation would just continue on the way it was just left me in total disbelief, how can someone think that it is ok to treat another person so terribly the way she had been treating me for so long now, and then think that I would just stay and suffer the abuse even more!!!

Your mother always laughed at me saying that no one would believe me if I tried to tell anyone what was happening and how I felt, I mean if I tried to tell any of my family or friends about being abused by my girlfriend everyone would think I was mad, no one would believe that a woman could damage a man so much would they?

And how could I tell anyone when I was intentionally separated from my support group over the last few years?

Your mother knew that by alienating me this way would prevent me from ever having been able to confide in my family and friends and she knew that the last time I had managed to have a decent conversation with anyone outside of our relationship was a long time ago, your mother would simply not allow me to talk to anyone other than her and all the time I had been cut off from my family and friends your mother had made it her mission to visit them all and tell her warped version of events to them, I had no idea your mother had been spreading her lies to all my family and friends covertly without my knowledge, she had carefully laid down a story where I was the bad guy and your mother was the victim of my bad behavior, she had made it impossible for me to get anyone to see the truth of what was really going on, I was thankful that last night my friends witnessed your mothers true self, I think this added to the strength I needed to leave.

Suddenly, I did have the courage, and I did leave.

As I put the key on the kitchen side and left the flat for what I thought would be the last time, I felt a great sense of relief wash over me, I felt safe at last that I didn't have to sit in the flat and be victimized by your mother any longer, I was free from her abuse, I had escaped her abusiveness.

I put all my stuff in my camper van and drove over to my friend's house, I hooked up the electricity to the van and I camped on my friends drive in my peaceful van for the next few months, my friends wife cooked me dinner every evening and I would sit with their family for an hour or so every evening in their home before retiring to my van to go to sleep.

I loved being in my van, the peaceful evenings, it was very comfortable. It had a comfy corner settee, a toilet shower room where I could have hot showers, a microwave and cooker to cook meals on and a fridge to store my food, and the double bed was dreamily comfy too.

All my love

Dad

CHAPTER THREE

Peace and Tranquility Ruined

All I want is a bit of peace and quiet T-Minus 27 months before your due date

June 1, 2020

Dear Eliza,

The peace I was enjoying didn't last long before your mother started messaging me. It had only been a few days since I left, she was trying to gain information on me from my social media, she was not on my social media at all, I had to remove her, as she was stalking my friends and causing trouble for me.

When your mother was on my social media, she would hunt through my feed to see if there was any information on there that she could use to attack me with, any little piece of information she could twist into using against me, anything that she could find to give her a reason to start an argument with. This was draining and exhausting, I became terrified of my family and friends tagging me in things.

If anyone tagged me in social events or places of interest the rows would always start with your mother telling me not to even think about me going to any of them, and accusations of other girls being there.

Your mother just had to know what I was doing in my life and attack me with the information she found out, and now I had left her she had been stalking my friends social media accounts trying to find the answer to the questions that burned inside her, she just had to know what I was doing, where I was going and where I was living, she had no idea of what arrangements I had made, she had no clue as to where I was living and she couldn't gain any information on what I was doing in my life and this was driving her crazy.

Truth be known, I wasn't doing anything other than going to work and coming back to my camper van at the end of the day, I wasn't in the mood to go out socializing, your mother had knocked the stuffing out of me and I just didn't want to go and socialize pretending to be ok when I really wasn't at all, I wanted to take some time out to heal myself a bit first before I attempted to do anything other than just breathe.

Your mother just wouldn't leave me alone, she had been approaching several of my friends directly by texting and messaging them to ask if any of them knew where I was and what I was doing and when she didn't get any information back from any of them, she was forced to message me directly.

She started off by asking if I was ok, and asked if I was coping ok, another tactic of hers when trying to find out about me, she would message being nice and asking after my welfare before her questions became more specific and more probing.

This is a tactic called "hoovering" she was trying to find out what I was doing, she wanted to know if I was going out and having fun and if I had met anyone else, but the ultimate aim of the tactic of hoovering is to get a victim to return back to their abuser all because the abuser needs to maintain the control over their victim.

Hoovering is a cat and mouse game that someone who abuses others needs to play as it feeds into their own ego, your mother didn't care about how I felt at all, it was all about how she felt, our whole time together had been all about your mothers moods, how she felt, what she wanted, what she wasn't happy with it was never about me at all, it never had been, the relationship with your mother was terribly one sided and that one side was heavily stacked on her side and not mine.

The messages I started to receive from your mother said she missed me, she loved me and wanted me to come back, she made promises of her changing and not being so horrible towards me, your mother said she would work on her behavior and her attitude and that she would not hurt me anymore, she then started messaging saying she couldn't cope without me and that if I loved her I would go back to her, I only ever received messages like this from your mother when she wanted something, she was "never" nice to me, all her messages were always abusive and horrible and this hoovering tactic is designed to play on a victims emotional responses, and your mother was excellent at doing this to me.

With this kind of emotional blackmail tactic being used on me, one where your mother knew I had no defense against, I lasted two months living in my van on my friends drive before I gave in to your mother and went back to living with her at the flat.

All my will power all my strength to resist your mother had left me and the moment I returned, all those promises your mother had made to me were broken, she was nice to me for less than a day before the old patterns of abuse started to reappear and she started to inflict even more hurt and pain on me than she had done before I left, I was made to feel even worse, I realized that going back to her turned out to be a massive mistake on my behalf, and I wished I had not gone back to your mother at all, I wished I had remained strong and listened to my friend and his wife who were telling me to not go back.

The next few months were torture for me, I was made to feel like my life wasn't worth anything at all, and that I was just being used to entertain your mothers' toxic needs, I was being used yet again as an emotional punch bag for your mother to take out her frustrations on yet again, nothing at all had changed, in fact things were made worse by going back. I felt like a ragdoll pulled backwards and forwards, my head couldn't cope with the emotions racing through it. I was overwhelmed with disappointment in myself, why did I go back?

All my love

Dad

CHAPTER FOUR

Why the Hell did I go back?

*Motocross, Madness and Mayhem T-Minus
26 months before your due date*

July 1, 2020

Dear Eliza,

It's summer time and I should be happy, but I am not, I am back in the same toxic mess I was before I left your mother, right back where I started from again, I can feel the life draining from me, the only fun I get now is to leave the house to go motocross with my friends, I used to take your mother and your brother with me but I find that mentally I just cannot cope with your mothers tantrums and drama sages any longer, I need to focus on motocross and riding my bike on the track, it's a dangerous sport and my head needs to be in the game and your mother makes that difficult with all the arguments she causes.

Your mother ridicules my riding abilities, she laughs at me and says I am shit, she tries to convince me to give it all up for her, your mothers says if I loved her that I would give this up because she is asking me to, she would scream and shout at me accusing me of loving motocross more than her and that I am choosing it over her, she would insult me and call me horrible names for wanting to do something I loved.

This is my hobby that I have enjoyed since I was a little boy, my dad got me a bike when I was 5 years old and we went to junior motocross events all over our local area, my dad got me hooked on it, and I loved the thrill, the smells of the track, I enjoyed the skill that was needed to ride a bike on rough terrain in all weather conditions, there was no way on earth I was giving all this up, I had bought all the gear I needed to participate in this sport over the years, I had the bike, the clothing, the van to get the bike to and from events, all the skills I had learnt over the years, you cannot just give this up in the blink of an eye.

This upset your mother, she wanted me to prove how much I loved her by giving up the one thing I loved doing, and when I wouldn't give it up, she used this to target me further, your mother always forced me to choose her over anything I wanted to do.

Everything I wanted to do was attacked by your mother and bashed down, everything I loved destroyed, I had sacrificed a lot for your mother over the years and this was the one thing that I was not prepared to sacrifice at all.

The rows going to motocross caused were unbelievable, from the moment I left the house to the moment I got back at the end of a race event I received message after message and abusive call after call, if I didn't reply to a message when your mother sent it, she would send many more abusive messages accusing me of having more fun there than at the flat with her, if I was riding when she called she would leave an abusive voice mail message, I could hear the hatred in her voice, sometimes she was ranting fast calling me all the names under the sun and other times she was speaking slow and threatening saying don't bother coming back to the flat because she had locked me out and thrown all my things outside for people to take! I got this treatment every time I attended a motocross event.

I lived in constant fear of returning, but every time I did return, I found your mother hadn't thrown any of my things outside at all, it was just empty threats to hurt me and keep me living in fear of what she may or may not do, she was breaking my head, I felt like I just wanted it all to end, I wanted your mother to stop hurting me like this but she never changed at all, she just continued doing this to me.

Every time I tried to talk to her about what she was doing to me she just laughed at me and called me a pussy then changed the conversation onto her instead.

I became numb to her threats and I began to stop taking it to heart, anything vile she threw at me I just took it, I let it wash over me, yes, it still hurt me but there was nothing I could do about it, I knew to never let your mother see she had hurt me, as this would only lead to further abuse in this way, so I learnt to just ignore her when she was ranting as I had no control over any of it I was totally powerless to it all. I tried to focus more on what I was doing at the time; this was one of my ways of coping with it all.

I knew your mother could not be reasoned with, she was totally unreasonable, and trying to reason with her was a total waste of my time.

It's funny when I think of the motto on my social media at the time when all this was going on, it said, "you have one life, live it" but I definitely wasn't living my life the way I wanted to be living it at all, in fact it was the total opposite, my life had become this daily hell that I didn't want to be living every day!

I am trying to get stronger when dealing with your mother, but I must admit failure here, she is very difficult to manage.

All my love

Dad

CHAPTER FIVE

Summer Is Ending and So Am I

Been kicked out AGAIN T-Minus 25 months before your due date

August 1, 2020

Dear Eliza,

I can feel myself shutting down, I am getting worse with every passing day, I can feel my mental health declining, your mother is having a party at the flat and has thrown me out saying she doesn't want me there, she is demanding I hand over my door key to her and told me not to come back until she says I can and lets me.

I don't feel like this flat is my home, I am constantly reminded that your mothers' name is on the tenancy agreement and that she can do anything she likes to me, she laughs at me when she says I have no rights at all and that I must do everything she says, she smirks at me when she says she owns me and there is nothing I can do about it.

In her true selfish twat style, she has dropped this on me with an hours' notice, she is shouting at me that I must get out and to hurry up and pack a bag you little prick. I have nowhere to go, she knows this, but she doesn't care about me, as usual your mother is only interested in her own selfish needs, I am lucky that I have my race van, so that is where I go.

I grab a few things and head out the door leaving my door key on the side, your mother smirking at me as I leave shouting "go on leave you cu@t and don't fu@king come back till I say you can"

As the door slams behind me I can hear your mother laughing hysterically, she does this thing where she tips her head back and laughs so loud, it really freaks me out, it gives me the feeling that she is completely insane, it really is unnerving and adds to me being terrified of her.

I am heading back to my van yet again, hurt and upset, I have tears rolling down my face, but no one sees this side of me, I just unlock the van and get inside, I drive off down the road to get some food supplies for however long I may be in the van again, I am never sure when your mother kicks me out of the flat, it could be one night or longer.

It's never long before your mother starts to message me with hurtful comments about how she owns the flat and me, how she has control over everything and I have no say what so ever, she puts laughing emojis on her messages but I don't reply, as I know if I reply she will just get worse and it will lead to me being unable to get back in the flat for longer, so I say nothing, I just read all the hurtful messages and sit in my van and cry where no one can see me.

I don't know how much more of this I can take Eliza, and yet, I don't know why I don't just leave, I don't have the strength to keep leaving and going back to your mother, I'm so worn out with all the emotional coming and going, I think your mother knows this, she knows I don't have the strength to leave her, she knows I will come back again when she says I can, she knows she holds the control over me. What I am beginning to struggle with is how I have allowed this to happen to me and why do I allow it to continue too?

Something I later discovered, I was in a "trauma bond" with your mother, my resistance and my self-esteem had been eroded by her to the point where I began to depend on her to give me orders and direct me in everything, I had become incapable of making any decisions, she had chipped away at me over the years and molded me into a completely different version of myself, a version that was easily manipulated into doing whatever she wanted me to do for her, then her vengeful attacks on me, calling me weak screaming at me that she had no respect for a man who allows a woman to walk all over him!

Even though my family and friends had seen so many changes in me over the years, they never for one moment knew what had caused all of these changes, I never permitted anyone to see the truth behind my pain, and I never told anyone of the deep rooted hurt inside of me, I just tried to bury it all and appear to be normal to the outside world, I didn't want people to know and I didn't want people asking questions, I wasn't strong enough to answer any of them. So, I just carried on covering up what was happening and making excuses for your mother's behavior so no one would know the depth of the abuse I was suffering I was hurt and embarrassed by it all, and I didn't know what to do anymore.

Because your mother had told her toxic lies to my family and friends and laughed at me saying no one would believe me if I ever tried to tell them what was going on it led to me just staying and trying to cope, I had no plan to be able to leave, I had no money as your mother made sure she took most of it, the loans she had taken out and put in my name ensured I had little to no money to myself, she knew I couldn't afford to rent anywhere!

I couldn't reason with her, I couldn't change her behavior towards me, I just sat and took everything she threw at me, I could feel myself getting deeper in with her with no way of ever getting out, I felt hopeless and could feel myself sinking lower all the time.

I had been skillfully moved to the point of not fighting back by a master manipulator and I had failed to see this until it was too late, and I was balls deep with no way of escaping at all.

I'm trying to work through all this pain inside of me,

All my love

Dad

CHAPTER SIX

Just Grin and Bare It

*Autum months are normally enjoyed by me T-
Minus 24 months before your due date*

September 1, 2020

Dear Eliza,

It is two years before you are meant to be born, I am trying so hard to stay positive but every time I try to do anything nice your mother just rips into me, bringing me down to her low level of self-loathing and self-hatred. I don't want to be made to feel like this, it just isn't right.

Your mother won't admit she has a problem, she won't go and get help, despite me asking for her to go and see a doctor. She deflects the blame for everything onto me, her normal phrases now are "if you didn't do that, I wouldn't have shouted at you" another favorite phrase of hers is "if you didn't make me angry, I wouldn't get so upset" and the worst saying of hers now that she uses for most things is "If you loved me, you would do as I asked without question".

Your mother never admits she started any of the arguments, they are all blamed on me, she has an excuse for everything she does, she always has a big story as to why she did something or why she said something, and it is always my fault.

I am at the point where I am just accepting the blame for things I know I haven't done or said, but it is easier to just accept your mothers' venomous accusations of wrongdoing, I have learnt there is no point trying to stand up for myself or in trying to make your mother see reason, she is incapable of accepting any blame for anything and you just cannot reason with an unreasonable person............... FACT!

Your mother falls out with people all the time, she is always engaged in some kind of trouble or drama with someone and its never your mothers' fault of course, it is always the fault of the other person never hers, she has moved her horses so many times now after falling out with the owners of the yards that they were being kept at that I have lost count.

You can take a horse to water, but
you can't make it drink

This phrase was first listed in 12th Century Proverbs
by a man named John Heywood in 1546, that man
knew back then that your mother would be trouble!

I am beginning to see that your mother has antisocial tendencies, and I fear that she will never accept any responsibility for any of her actions, she will always deflect the blame onto others rather than herself. No one can make your mother see the error of her ways................ no one, not even her own mother, your grandmother.

The amount of times we have been sitting at your grandmothers' house when your mother has said something awful to me in front of her, your grandmother has told your mother off for talking to me so awfully, then asked me if I can handle your mother! I mean, what kind of person says that about their own daughter?

A person who has witnessed your mother's atrocious behavior and knows exactly what she is like towards other people, that's who.

We call people like these "enablers" they not only ignore bad behaviour, they actually encourage it!

All my love

Dad

CHAPTER SEVEN

Deflated Sails

*Your Mother's birthday T-Minus 22
months before your due date.*

November 12, 2020

Dear Eliza,

This whole year has been spent defending myself to your mother, even her birthday has not seen any let up in her animosity towards me, we haven't arranged to go out anywhere and the boots I bought for her and wrapped up really nice, the boots she desperately wanted because they were just so lovely and her life would end if she didn't have them, have been carelessly thrown to the back of the cupboard, another thing I got wrong!!

Your mother is making me out to be a big fat liar and a big fat failure, more ridicule for me, more abuse and false accusations from your mother, I can't even get her birthday present right.

I gave up.

This is all I have to say on the matter of your mother's birthday I just don't have the words to describe what happened!

All my love

Dad

CHAPTER EIGHT

Christmas Cheer Tis the Season
To Be Jolly Fa La La La La

December 25, 2020, Christmas Day T-Minus
21 months before your due date.

Dear Eliza,

I decided to visit my mother today on Christmas Day, that was wrong, as your mother wanted to come with me, despite telling me the night before that there was no way she was coming to my mother's house because she didn't like my mother, even though she never told my mother that, so I left the flat early to visit my family and exchange presents in the hope of not causing any arguments, but yet again I discovered no matter what I do its wrong in your mothers' eyes, I'm really beginning to lose the will to live here.

As I was sat having a cup of tea with my mother, my phone started to ring, it was your mother, she had woken up and seen that I wasn't in the flat, and as expected she was demanding to know where I was, shouting down the phone, accusing me of seeing another woman on Christmas Day, my mother looked at me in shock, she could hear your mother screaming and shouting at me down the phone, I left the house and stepped outside into the garden to take the call, just to save all my family hearing me being abused and belittled by your mother. I really couldn't face my family hearing what was being said.

This happened so often now that my family were aware of what was happening to me, they had been witnesses to these abusive phone calls many times over the last few months but today I just didn't want to do this in front of my family, I stepped outside to prevent your toxic mother infecting the good cheer that was inside my parents' house, I didn't want to expose my family to what I have to suffer it's just not fair, and I didn't want to be the one responsible for ruining their Christmas happiness by them all having to listen to your mothers' venomous words.

My mother and father stood and watched me through the kitchen window, they saw me trying to reason with your mother and calm her down, they could see I was uncomfortable and agitated by the abusive phone call. Your mother was ridiculing me calling me a mummy's boy and saying that I was weak for running back to my "mummy" all the time.

Your mother was demanding I come back to the flat so we could go over to your grandmothers' for the day, I tried so hard to speak but your mother was firing off so many words at me that I just couldn't get a word in edge ways, and I couldn't reason with her at all, I stood in the garden just listening to your mother verbally assaulting me over and over again, telling me what a failure I am, insulting me in every way she could think of, screaming abuse at me, until she eventually had finished with abusing me and she hung up.

Even though the call ended, my trauma caused by it didn't,

I put my phone away, I hated the fact that your mother could reach me and get to me where ever I was, I had nowhere that I could escape from her, I went back inside and my family could see I was visibly shaken and really upset, the topic of conversation quickly moved to why I hadn't left your mother and why I was still there, and I had no answers to this at all, I wanted to leave, but I just couldn't, I was becoming terrified of your mother and was fearful of what she would do, she always threatened to ruin my life if I ever left her and I didn't have the courage to challenge her on this matter.

So, I stayed with her.

All my love

Dad

CHAPTER NINE

Ending the Year being held captive.

December 31, 2020, New Years Eve T-Minus
21 months before your due date.

Dear Eliza,

Your mother decided that we were not going out tonight, she wasn't in the mood, she is never in the mood to go out anywhere, she just sits on the settee all the time now insulting other people for having fun, I can see her jealous hateful side so clearly, she is envious of other people enjoying their lives while she sits at the flat slagging other people off, your mother never wants to leave the flat, but she becomes extremely aggressive and abusive if I want to leave the flat, so I sit here feeling isolated and trapped forced to listen to her constant moaning and complaining.

Its New Years Eve we should be out celebrating having fun, but instead we stayed in sitting on the settee watching the rubbish on the tv, your mother was doom scrolling through her social media accounts getting upset at everyone else out celebrating having fun bringing in the new year with a bang, carefully watching me while I looked at my social media, your mother was watching every comment I made on a post and the things I was liking, your mother demanding to know whose posts I was commenting on.

I was dreading receiving the normal family and friends Happy New Year messages as I knew your mother would become jealous of every single message I received and without fail she became aggressive with me when my phone started receiving these messages at midnight, I wasn't even allowed to receive well wishes from my family and friends, something that everyone else got with no issues and because of how your mother was I never sent any Happy New Year messages this year, I just didn't want the trouble of sending them to people.

I had started to put my phone on silent mode so your mother couldn't hear when people messaged me, she was always watching to see if my phone lit up and demanded to know who was messaging me, this was one of the worst new years' eve evenings I had ever had in my whole life.

I decided that next year I would do something fun, that could either be with or without your mother, I had made my mind up that I was not going to sit at home switching between awkward silences to full blown arguing next year, and that was it, my mind was made up about it, I wanted to enjoy my life and that was just not happening being with your mother.

I think this was the time I started to think about how I was going to leave your mother for good, I needed to come up with some kind of plan to let her down gently but also make her see that our relationship has stopped being healthy for both of us a long time ago and it would be better for us both to end the toxic mess we had gotten ourselves into. But I knew your mother would have trouble accepting this and leaving her was not going to be easy.

Watch this space!

All my love

Dad

CHAPTER TEN

New Year New Mindset, Same Crap!

*January 1, 2021, Happy New Year T-Minus
20 months before your due date.*

Dear Eliza,

Even though it is the first day of a new year, I am still upset and miserable, my anxiety is through the roof living with your mother, and I think I am now suffering with depression, my family and friends and even your grandmother have all asked me how I put up with your mothers behavior and they all ask me why I haven't left her yet. I am starting to ask myself the same thing more and more with each passing day now.

> I know I should leave your mother, but I
> can't find the right time to do it.

I can't wait to leave for work, it is the only escape I get now, and even despite your mother constantly ringing my phone and messaging all day accusing me of anything trivial that she can use to start an argument with, today it was not tidying up before I left for work or not doing the washing up, even though I did do these things, I do feel a bit resentful some days, I get upset with myself for taking responsibility for the flat when your mother constantly reminds me that it is "her" flat and not mine, that her name is on the tenancy not mine, she is such a hypocrite, she doesn't want me having anything nice but she is happy for me to pay for it all.

Your mother uses me to get the things she wants in her life, and she uses my money to get these things too, she doesn't want to pay for anything herself, so she uses me and my money, everything is about money with her, she constantly reminds me that she is better than me because she earns more money than me, and yet I pay for most things and she is always in debt? How is that even possible.

Your mother demands to know how much money I get but she never tells me how much money she gets, she never lets me know how much money she spends or what she spends her money on, she laughs at me when she says, "my money is my own and your money is mine also".

I sit here wondering what I have done to make your mother treat me so badly, what have I said? I go over things in my mind, I can't find how we got to this point, I can't put my finger on what lead us to become like this, and I sit here in total confusion over how I allowed this to happen to me, I feel so deflated, like a sailboat with no wind in its sails, it's not going anywhere fast.

I feel like my life has been taken away from me.

I don't feel like myself anymore, I feel like I am living in someone else's body and mind, this is not me! This is not the real me! I am no longer the real me, I have been pushed and forced into becoming a different version of myself, I sound crazy saying this, but it's true! I am no longer the person I used to be before meeting your mother, I am this empty shell pretending to be me, I don't like feeling like this, I have always seen a way through difficult times in my life, but all I see right now is total darkness, I don't have answers for things anymore, I can't see a way forward and most of all I can't see a way out of it all either.

I can feel myself sinking deeper into this darkness, all the things I used to enjoy doing, all my hobbies no longer bring me joy, I don't care either way if I do them or not.

The only tiny bit of happiness I get now is being away from the flat and away from your mother, I have reached a point where I don't want to be in the same room as her anymore, but I still stay with her. I cannot understand why I stay.

One of my friends called your mother a "narc"
today, I had no idea what he meant.

The whole month of the New Year has been hell, I can't do a thing right in your mothers' eyes, I am blamed for everything that happens in her life! I just accept her accusations now as I know trying to stand up for myself will just make her even angrier, so I just let her abusive words wash over me like a wave.

All my love

Dad

CHAPTER ELEVEN

Darkness is falling all around me

February 1, 2021, Things are no better T-Minus 19 months before your due date.

Dear Eliza,

We are into the second month of the year and things are no better, I have approached the subject of your mother and me parting ways and living our lives separately, but your mother doesn't want me to leave, she says she cannot afford to pay all the bills in the flat if I go and that she needs me to keep paying for things.

I have planted a seed in your mothers mind, I am waiting for this seed to grow now, us splitting up needs to be your mothers idea and not mine, she knows things aren't working, neither of us are happy, and we are at a point where we can no longer hide this from ourselves and the outside world, I was hoping that your mother would see sense and agree to part ways amicably.

Finally your mother agreed that our relationship was just not working, and that we both needed to have space from each other, your mother suggested that I move into the spare room and pay her rent to stay at the flat, I must admit I never saw this one coming, yet again your mother has chosen an option in our break up that suites her needs and not mine, yet again my feelings have not been considered here and the whole situation has been twisted to play your mother out as the honorable one in all of this, with her family and friends saying how great she is at considering me and not kicking me out but instead allowing me to remain at the flat.

Your mother was reveling in the attention she received with her family and friends saying how lovely and kind she is to allow me to stay there and if it was them they would have kicked me out in an instant, then going on to say how your mother doesn't owe me anything as it is her flat not mine, here it is again, me being made out to be the bad guy and your mother playing the role of the hero yet again, I am getting sick and tired of forever being the villain in your mothers stories, every time I am told I am the bad guy it crushes me.

I tried to think of this in a positive way, it was really hard for me to attempt to play the long game in all of this, I was being abused by third parties now as well as your mother, but I remembered your mother always saying to me that if I tried to leave her she would make my life a living hell, I had no idea of what she was capable of, so I agreed to move to the spare room, I thought I could then begin to think of ways in which I could leave the flat and your mother for good.

I made the mistake of thinking your mother would get used to us not being together anymore and that she would get fed up with me being in her way, I thought that she would reach a point where she would get bored of not being able to antagonize me any longer as I come in from work and just go straight to my room.

I was no longer sitting in the front room with her at all, I just sit on my bed now, but I was trying to get her to see that we had nothing left between us and to just let me go, your mother knew I was terrified to leave her; I had to convince her in some way that this was nothing to do with me at all and that is was all to do with what she wanted, so I sat and waiting for the day that your mother told me to leave.

But how was I going to get her to do that? Your mother had isolated me from my family and friends over the years, so much so that I didn't have anyone I could talk to about any of what was going on, my family and friends knew things at home were bad, but they never knew quite how bad things were in reality, and the advice they all gave me was to just leave, thinking that my nightmare would end the moment I left your mother, but they were all wrong, my nightmare would not end there, and I knew it too.

I just knew that your mother would make trouble for me if I was the one to end it all, I couldn't see any way out of my situation, so I stayed in the spare room, just waiting until the day arrived that your mother said to get out, I had to put up with your mother going through my things, going through my van, your mother would sneak into my room in the middle of the night when she thought I was asleep and try to get hold of my phone, she managed to do it some nights too, she went through my phone to see who I was talking to, she was angry at me for talking to other people about our situation, your mother didn't want other people knowing what was going on, she wanted to be the one telling people stories of our relationship filling peoples' heads with lies about how great she was and how bloody awful I was, your mother threatened me to keep my mouth shut and not to talk to anyone behind her back about our relationship, your mother told me that if she found out I had been taking to anyone about her she would ruin me.

Your mother started messaging my friends, asking if they had been speaking to me and asked what the conversations had been about. Your mother was paranoid that people would see her for who she truly was and not the false outer image your mother was projecting on everyone. Your mother worked so hard, getting people to believe she was a nice person and that I was the one in the wrong, she gossiped about me to anyone who would listen, and she was very creative in her lies about me being awful, she was a very convincing liar.

Your mother had isolated me from the outside world, she had shut me away like a dirty little secret in the spare room at the flat, still trying to exercise total control over me, I was being held like a prisoner of her own delusions, and anything I said or did that did not align with her wishes was smashed down instantly, I was being threatened and coerced into behaving the way she wanted me to behave, my personal identity had been erased over the last few years, the version of me that existed before we got together no longer existed, I was being forced into becoming this different version of myself that just wasn't me, I had this constant darkness inside me now, it never left me, it just grew darker.

Your mother had sunk her claws into me in so many ways, I felt like a puppet with her pulling all the strings, she had total control over me, she controlled what I said, who I saw, she demolished my support group, she stopped me going out anywhere other than to go to work, she had taken loans out in my name leaving me to pay the monthly instalments on them all and I couldn't hand these loans back to her because she was clever enough to register them all in my name and I was too naive to see what she was doing at the time.

I had been led into trusting your mother and now I was financially liable for everything she had set me up for, your mother was terrible with money, she was always in debt herself even though she ridiculed me for earning more money than me, but she never had any money which I found strange! Your mother sent me a picture of her sitting on the settee at home on her laptop, she sent this picture with a comment saying she gets to sit at home on her arse all day and still earns more money than me, your mother took great delight in insulting me and my manhood at every opportunity she could.

Even though I knew it was wrong to be talked into taking loans out in my name, and I know I should have said no at the time, but I just couldn't say no to your mother, she had this way of convincing you that it was the right thing to do, and that I should be the one to do it for her too, she would insult me saying, if I was a real man I would pay this for her or get this for her, she has trapped me into staying with her, she knew I couldn't afford to move out and pay rent anywhere, I was stuck and I had no way of ever getting out.

I sank lower into a deep depression.

All my love

Dad

CHAPTER TWELVE

Motocross Season has Started

March 31, 2021, A whole month of nothings T-Minus 18 months before your due date.

Dear Eliza,

I have spent the whole month trying desperately to think of a way that would enable me to leave your mother and the flat, I hate coming home from work and going straight to my room, I feel like a kid again coming home from school, I didn't like being a teenager locked away in my room I was always outside with my friends, we were always out having fun and doing things together, and now I was sat all alone by myself in the spare room isolated from family and friends with no one to talk to and no one to care for me.

I had never felt so alone in my whole life and now I was sitting here feeling terrible about my life and my choices I had made, mainly the choices involving your mother, with every passing day I became more isolated and more upset, it became harder for me to leave the house to go to work every day, my body felt ten times heavier than normal and I just didn't see a way out of how I was feeling or a safe way out of escaping my current situation at the flat with your mother.

Motocross season had started again and I found it great to get the bike out and get back on the race track with all my motocross friends, it felt great being away from the flat and away from your mother, but the messages I started to receive once I arrived at the tracks were always the same, abusive, horrible put downs, assaulting my character, accusing me of being with another woman, or lying, to add to it all your mother would be messaging other motocross friends that were also there asking them if I was really there and if I was with anyone. I just couldn't escape the abuse no matter where I went.

Even though our relationship had ended I was still tied to your mother, and I was still experiencing her vileness in everything I did.

My phone was going off constantly, every time it made a noise, I began to get anxious, I knew it was your mother demanding answers to her never ending rude questions, I couldn't stop myself reading through the abuse, it was like I was just as addicted to reading her messages as she was at sending them to me, I read her hurtful comments accusing me of caring for motocross more than I did for her, of never having cared for her at all the whole time we were together, I felt that this is what she should have been saying to your brothers father and not me! I began to get angry at your mother for punishing me for something I never did to her. I was getting sick of being blamed for things I never said, and I never did.

Attack after attack, assault after assault, the verbal abuse just continued with no signs of ever stopping! I felt incredibly hurt by it all, the accusations of not caring, the accusations of lying and cheating it was all chipping away at my self-confidence until I just sat there and didn't care what was being said to me anymore, I had been convinced that I was a bad person and that I deserved to be treated this way, your mother had made me believe all the lies she was telling everyone about me, how for the last few years I had been accused of everything bad under the sun until the day I actually became convinced that I deserved it all. My whole sense of reality was crumbling faster than I could try to hold it together and I couldn't stop myself from breaking.

I sat at motocross in my van, crying, I should have been working on my bike and making sure it was track ready, but all I could do was sit and cry.

When did I become this version of myself? How had I let your mother reduce me to this? I didn't do anything wrong, why was I being punished so badly?

I just wanted it all to stop.

All my love

Dad

CHAPTER THIRTEEN

I can feel myself breaking

April 30, 2021, I need counselling and therapy, I need help T-Minus 17 months before your due date.

Dear Eliza,

I'm totally broken, your mother has convinced me that I am not a worthy person, that I don't deserved a happy life or nice things, I am being told every day that I am stupid, that I am an idiot, I am being led to believe that there is no hope for me, my strength I have been using to get me through each day is starting to leave me, and I have no hope of it every coming back, I know I am broken, I know I need to leave for my own mental health and my own personal safety, and yet I still stay, trapped like an animal in a cage with no way of getting out and no hope of anyone coming to rescue me.

I dream of someone removing me from this awful situation, just coming in and taking me away, someone who is caring and kind that can see how much pain I am in.

I stay in a place that I know I am not loved, and I know I am not wanted, and yet I don't have the strength to leave, I have been battered into submission by the relentless abuse I have been receiving from your mother, her only use of me if for my money to pay her bills and to be there for when she needs someone to take her anger out on, someone to deflect all her failings onto.

All self-respect I had for myself is gone, I believe that I am neither good nor bad, that I just am! I know I am alive, as I am moving my body around and I am breathing but I feel so numb inside of me. The happiness I once held for the world is gone, how do I cope every day feeling like this, how do I repair myself, how can I move away from all of this.

The most important question now is, why don't I just leave, how can I get together enough money and support to leave and start my life over again.

It feels like someone has nailed my feet to the floor, I am incapable of moving my feet in the direction of the door. No one will ever love me like this, no one will ever want to be with me like this.

I don't know what to do, it's like being stuck in deep mud.

All my love

Dad

CHAPTER FOURTEEN

I must find a way to get stronger

May 31, 2021, I made it to another month T-Minus 16 months before your due date.

Dear Eliza,

I made it another month, I can't believe I am still here in this flat living in the spare room with your mother, I have become so used to getting up and going to work and coming home again and just returning to what I have come to call my prison cell.

I cling to my mobile phone, it has become my lifeline to the outside world, a tool I can use to reconnect with people outside of my four walls, I have been purposely avoiding our mother, she hasn't spoken to me for a few days, I can hear her crashing around the flat, sometimes she jiggles the bedroom door handle and laughs loudly from the other side of the door, she doesn't enter the room, she just laughs and walks off again.

I am being tortured, but at least I am speaking with others now on the phone, I even started a dating profile online and put in my details, normal girls are messaging me on there, it is refreshing to be able to talk to pretty young ladies who are genuinely interested in me, they are asking questions trying to get to know me, and I am answering their questions and asking questions of my own.

I sit here dreaming of finding a young lady who wants me for who I am, just enjoying each other's company and just doing normal things that normal couples do together with no emotional or verbal attacks being launched at me. I want to find a place of peace and harmony where I can begin to feel safe and work on repairing the damage your mother has inflicted on me, I'm asking a lot of my next partner, I need a woman who totally understands my situation and doesn't judge me for what

I allowed to happen to me, I need a really caring person who has a strong character who will be able to help me move forward, I know your mother is not going to tolerate me seeing other women once I move out, she will stalk me and any women I see in the future I just know this will happen because she has done this to me now for quite some time, it has become a habit for your mother that she is incapable of breaking, she needs professional help with her issues but she will never admit she needs help or that she has done anything wrong at all.

One can dream.

All my love

Dad

CHAPTER FIFTEEN

I have the breaking strain of a Kit-Kat

June 1, 2021, Time for some brutal honesty T-Minus 15 months before your due date.

Dear Eliza,

Your mother came into my room last night while I was sleeping, she went through my mobile phone; after going through my phone, she spent the night messaging all the people I had been speaking to. I had told your mother that I had a dating profile and was looking to meet other women, but she didn't like that I had done this, your mother made a fake dating profile with the same dating app that I had joined and she started to message my online dating profile, your mother also got one of her friends to create a fake dating profile and message me too, I knew straight away it was your mother, so I deleted the account.

Despite your mother and me no longer being in a relationship together she still doesn't want me to find someone else to be happy with, your mother wants me to stay at the flat and not leave it, and she still wants to dictate what I can do with my life, she loves to see me upset and miserable, it's intoxicating to her.

I couldn't stay there anymore, I moved out and started living in my camper van again, I was there for four weeks and the whole time I received messages from your mother saying she would try harder to make our relationship work and convinced me to go back to her at the flat, but once again, I allowed myself to be talked into going back, with the promise of things being different this time and that your mother would change her ways, well she didn't, and now I was living in her bedroom again with her, I think it was her way of making sure I wasn't on my phone talking to other women, she didn't want me to escape her clutches, she had no intention of ever letting me go.............. ever!

In your mother's eyes, I was her property, I belonged to her and her alone, no one else would ever have me.

I'm crumbling! I feel such shame for allowing this to happen to me over and over again, little did I know at the time, but his is known as an "abuse cycle" this is where an abuser will not allow a victim to escape their clutches, they use any means available to them to keep their victim locked to them.

All my love

Dad

CHAPTER SIXTEEN

*I'm barely holding onto the merry
go round I now call my mind*

*July, August, September 2021 – T-Minus
14 months before your due date.*

Dear Eliza,

What can I say about these three months being back with your mother? I hated it, every single minute of the time spent with her, we were still not talking to each other, days and nights spent sitting in total silence, your mother was not in the mood to communicate with me at all, this is another tactic called "stone walling" a tactic used to make a victim feel so bad about themselves, it is designed to convince a person that they are not worthy of loving, creating a feeling of abandonment whilst still being in a relationship with someone, it is vile and cruel and I hated being ignored and silenced, and your mother was using this tactic to punish me for leaving her again.

I felt so helpless, I wasn't allowed out of the flat for any reason other than to go to work, I wasn't allowed to speak with family or friends, and my mobile was being heavily guarded by your mother.

I couldn't live like this any longer, I needed to leave, and yet here I was still here!

I hated myself for being so weak, and for not being able to find a way out of this toxic mess I was in, I hated the fact that every time I managed to leave your mother that I always ended up going back to her, I knew now that things were never going to change.

All the times I had left your mother only to return again after she had promised me she would change, I now knew that your mother never had any intentions of changing, I had given her so many chanced to change over the last six years we had been together and she never made any lasting changes, in fact it wasn't long before she went back to being awful, I came to see that your mother is a toxic person, she has always been this way and she will always remain this way too. I stopped examining myself at this time and began focusing more on examining your mother, the way she fell out with everyone around her, the way she never had a good word to say about anyone, she always had an excuse to hand if she had a falling out with someone, or she lost her job for whatever reason, your mother had lost her job a few times since we had been together, she never seemed to be able to hold down a job for long, and the reason for her having to leave was always someone else's fault, never your mothers at all.

I met your mother when we were working for the same company, your mother worked as a scheduler, and I was one of the plumbers at the company, your mother was let go for theft, the manager said your mother had stolen a book of HETAS Certificates and this book cost a lot of money, your mother was the last one to sign this book out and it had gone missing, not only had this book gone missing but a second one had too, and your mother was the only one who had access to them both.

A massive row ensued, resulting in your mother being let go from the company, once the manager discovered your mother and me were dating, I was also let go from the company two weeks later too!!!

Your mother lied to me saying that the manager had been picking on her for the whole time she had worked there and that he was looking for an excuse to fire her.

I never forgave your mother for this!

And I hated myself for not leaving your mother at the time and for sticking up for her too! She cost me my job and my reputation at a place I had worked for for over 10 years since leaving school, but I was tied in with your mother and I was deemed by my boss as being guilty by association, he let me go saying that he couldn't trust me if I was with your mother.

Love always

Dad

CHAPTER SEVENTEEN

And I am Out AGAIN

October 2021, I got kicked out of the flat AGAIN
T-Minus 11 months before your due date.

Dear Eliza,

Your mother kicked me out of the flat and took my front door key off me AGAIN, she told me she was throwing a party with all her friends and that I wasn't invited and had to leave for the weekend, your mother told me that her friends didn't like me and that I wasn't welcome at all.

I felt incredibly hurt by your mother saying this, I had been kicked out by your mother yet again and I couldn't get back in to get any of my stuff as she had taken the door key off me, her usual tactic, so I couldn't come in the flat while she was doing whatever it was that she was doing and didn't want me to see.

I had nowhere to go at such short notice other than my van again, but this time I had one of my motocross friends approach me regarding what was happening with your mother, now I didn't say anything to anyone, how could I, I didn't have the time to say anything to anyone as it was sprung on me at short notice yet again, this friend of mine was on your mothers social media and was in contact with her via mobile phone too, he seemed to know all about the kind of weekend your mother was having at the flat and offered me a place to stay at his house for the weekend, I didn't even question him approaching me, and I didn't ask how he knew what was going on between me and your mother, I just gladly accepted his offer of sleeping in his spare room so I had somewhere solid to stay.

While I was staying at my friend's house I told them the truth as I was tired of lying for your mother, and they advised me to just pack my things and leave, my friends offered me their spare room until I could get on my feet, but I knew I couldn't afford to pay them any rent, so I politely declined their kind offer, plus another reason for not wanting to stay with them was that they were in direct contact with your mother and they would report back everything I was doing to her, and she knew their address too.

I would never have felt comfortable staying at their house when I knew your mother would have her personal spies to take notes on my every movement for her. Your mother liked involving other people in her web of lies, it made her feel powerful having all these people reporting to her with information, like a general in an army gaining intel.

It was a few days later when your mother finally called me to say I could go back inside the flat, at which point I had had enough of all the yoyoing with my mental health, I knew I was finally done with all the bad behaviors towards me, and I felt a new courage rising inside me, a courage that I just knew would help me to leave for good.

What your mother didn't realize was that this time by kicking me out of the flat she thought she held the upper hand in the situation, and your mother thought I would just go running back again like the weak person she accused me of being. This time, by kicking me out of the flat for what I now called "the last time she is ever doing that to me" she had pushed a button inside of me that I thought had disappeared forever and that button was called "hope" by staying with my friends, I got to see that they were concerned for me, and that they were offering to help me get away from your mother, they offered me a life line of hope and it has given me the best feeling I had had in a very long time, and it made me think to myself that there are people out there on my side, that the lies your mother was feeding me were just that, lies! She had been bluffing all along about my family and friends thinking I was an idiot and that no one liked me, your mother had also led me to believe that no one outside of our relationship would ever help me to escape from her.

Staying with my friends made me see that what your mother had been saying to me was bullshit, and that my family and friends didn't think so little of me, in fact it was the total opposite, so from then on, I started turning everything your mother said to me the other way round.

This tactic was mentioned to me by one of my great friends who I had been talking to, she knew I was feeling low and offered some counselling advice, this was my turning point, and although it started to make me mentally stronger I still was not brave enough to take the plunge and leave your mother for good, but it did start me thinking in a different way to how I had been thinking lately, and this method was starting to help me undo all the damage your mother had done to me over the last few years.

So, every time your mother said something nasty, I turned it into something good, when she said things like "everyone hates me" I turned it into "everyone loves me" and I started to flip her statements on their head, I never said anything to her mind, I knew she would laugh at me and get angry so I just kept this to myself, I found humor in what I was doing, for the first time in ages, I was starting to feel happier in myself, instead of apologizing all the time, I started saying thank you instead.

Another tactic to use given to me by my great friend, she said, instead of apologizing for being late, say thank you for waiting for me, she banned me from saying the word sorry for a week and told me I had to replace any apologies with thank you instead!

So simple and yet so effective

I found that I started to find tiny slithers of happiness in all the things I was doing again, and I found that I didn't carry around the deep feelings of shame and guilt about myself, I was starting to thank people more, and their responses were amazing, who would have thought that one simple change in your routine could bring about such massive changes.

I was starting to feel good about myself again.

I'm working on myself for a change

All my love

Dad

CHAPTER EIGHTEEN

Hope

*November 2021 My lifeline T-Minus 10
months before your due date.*

Dear Eliza,

I have started talking to all my family and friends again, I reached out to them and started reconnecting, I felt that I needed to, there is nothing left for me at the flat, being honest with myself there never was, it was your mothers flat in her name, she always reminded me of this, I need to start rebuilding my relationships with my family and friends that I have lost touch with since I have been with your mother, these relationships I am reestablishing and recreating with my family and friends are now forming part of my support group, these are the people who will start to help me repair the emotional damage inside me and will start advising me on how I should be putting myself back together.

I have spent a lot of time sitting with my family over this month, Christmas is edging closer, I am not really looking forward to spending it at the flat with your mother who I already know will be in the foulest of moods. Before we even get to the Christmas period, I just know your mother will be moody and depressing, she will be attacking me relentlessly like she has done all the previous Christmases in the past, I had made a promise to myself last Christmas and New Year that I was determined to have fun this year and spend more time with my family, I just wanted something better for myself this year and by talking to my family more, they have convinced me that I deserve so much better than this awful treatment from your mother.

My mother said I could live with her and my dad; they have a spare room that can be made available to me, my mother told me that I am welcome to stay there for as long as I like. The thought of escaping for good this time has left me feeling happy. I had forgotten how to feel happy; I had become used to just feeling miserable all the time and been convinced by your mother that I just didn't deserve to be happy.

Your mother could feel things changing inside of me, she knew I was becoming happier the more time I spent away from her and the flat and the more time I spent with my family the happier I became in myself, and your mother didn't like this new happier me that she saw emerging.

Your mother became moody and distant like she didn't know what to do about my newfound happiness, your mother hated to see me with my family, it really did anger her, she started to spend a lot of time over at your grandmothers' house, it was as if she was in competition with me going to see my family.

I didn't question it at all, in all honesty I was glad of the peace every time your mother left the flat. I could breathe again; I felt safe, I could sit and relax with no worries of me saying or doing something wrong in your mothers' eyes that would anger her and start a new argument that would go of for days.

I can feel the dynamics shifting now, and so can your mother too, we both know this is the end of the road for our relationship that there will be no coming back from this now, we had to both admit that and just go our own separate ways.

We are approaching the end of another year, and I am still sitting in the flat, but at least now your mother is leaving the flat more and giving me the much-needed peace I required, I need to keep hold of what little bit of sanity I have left, I can now see a way forward out of this mess for me.

The time I had alone in the flat while your mother was out allowed me to revisit our time together and I found myself going over the relationship from the start right up until where we were today, how had I reached a point in my life where I was beginning to break? mentally I knew I couldn't hold myself together anymore, I could feel myself slipping further and further into a darkness inside myself, one that I couldn't escape from, a darkness that I had become accustomed to living in with your mother, an accepted way of life that I had just begun to live every day, a pattern I was just living and accepting without trying to change it anymore, I had stopped trying to stand up for myself and the fight I had inside me before had just gone, I had nothing left of myself that I could actually relate to anymore.

I found myself thinking about how I used to sit in my work van in laybys wondering how the hell I was going to reverse my situation and undo all the pain I was now feeling, I had worked so hard at trying to please your mother and keep her happy, but it didn't matter what I did for her it was never enough but in my efforts to make your mother happy I had lost my grip on my own happiness, somehow I had let go of my happiness and sacrificed it all to a cause that I thought was way more important than my own needs.

How can I calm the demons that I now have in my head. I wondered how we had ended up like this as it wasn't always this way, when I first met your mother things were better, she was happier and we did lots of fun things together, we would arrange days out in my camper van, go to fun places and just kick back and be happy.

We could talk for hours, and your mother just seemed to understand me in every way. I started to go over when we first met, and how we got together, we had a friendship first before we started dating, we met at work, the one where I lost my job due to the manager claiming your mother had stolen company property, she was the new scheduler, she used to joke with me about how she had total control over my working day, and that she could keep loading jobs on me to keep me busy with no breaks, she allocated the work to me and I just went and did those jobs, your mother had worked for the company for about three months before we started dating each other, all that time we had chatted throughout the day, it wasn't until she moved into a new property she was renting and asked me to do some plumbing work for her, I went over to fix a radiator for her, then I just started helping your mother with lots of little things until eventually we just started to date each other.

I didn't really know too much about your mother until she started working at my company, and when she was accused of theft I didn't know what to believe, she had convinced me that my boss was persecuting her and that he had it in for her, your mother said he was picking on her and bullying her, I instantly felt protective towards her and I defended her to my boss, it was my defending her that got me sacked, thinking back now it was ludicrous that I trusted your mothers word having known her only three months over my boss who I had worked for for 10 years, I can see now why he let me go, I had chosen the wrong side to defend and it cost me my job.

I went over in my mind how in the beginning things seemed fine with your mother, but then she began to change, a darkness started to appear inside of her, she began to change in herself, the things in me she once found attractive, she now began to pick at. This was subtle to begin with, and over the last two years it became more frequent until every day was torture, I couldn't do a thing right in her eyes, I was always wrong, and I was blamed for everything that was going wrong in her life.

Over time I became anxious and terrified to say or do anything, it was a relief when I could leave the house to go to work, every morning I would sneak out of the house trying not to make your mother aware of the fact that I was leaving for work, but she would always be lying in wait to catch me, she would deliver her daily "I am so shit" speech to me before I left the flat every day, just to make sure there was no way I could feel good about myself at all, and to ensure that I felt awful the whole day that I was away from her too, she topped up my shit feelings by continually sending abusive messages she knew this would ensure that my feelings of worthlessness would last the whole day until I returned back to the flat again at the end of my working day, because having fun and being happy was not allowed for me, it was allowed for your mother, but not for me.

I went over how lots of things were not allowed for me, like how I wasn't allowed to visit my friends, or go on nights out socializing, I wasn't allowed to show happiness or laugh and smile, I wasn't allowed to defend myself or express an opinion of my own, I wasn't allowed to make any decisions on my life and I wasn't allowed to make a move without the permission of your mother being gained, my life was now being lived in terror.

I had gone from being my own person to being totally controlled and dominated by your mother. Every move tracked like a criminal with a data tag on. My phone was heavily monitored by your mother, she read every message I received and looked at all the calls I had made and received, I was not questioned about my day upon my return home from work each day..... I was interrogated to the point of mental exhaustion, our conversations were no longer a two way exchange of information, they had moved to a more one sided need to know my every move kind of conversation, and it didn't stop there once I had recounted my whole days movements to your mother then came the double questioning like she was trying to catch me out on something, your mother would go over what I said about something, she would pick it to pieces and then put all the information back together again, like picking apart a story then trying to test you on what you said, talking with your mother was exhausting.

After having the space and peace to run through all this again in my mind without being constantly terrorized by your mother I had come to realize that I no longer wished to live my life this way, I would no longer tolerate this kind of treatment towards me, its abuse, classed as "domestic abuse" and "domestic violence" this kind of abuse doesn't have to mean being beaten up physically, walking around with cuts and bruises, it can also include mental and emotional abuse too, and I had been subjected to domestic abuse now for over two years.

I no longer wanted to arrive home from work to a mood that I couldn't predict, a mood that could range from deathly silent treatment to terrorizing rage attacks, I no longer wanted to try to second guess this every day, I didn't want to enter the flat as quietly as I could to avoid upsetting your mother and causing a row, a row that I was always left in total confusion as to what I had done to start it in the first place, in all honestly looking back now, I know that I didn't cause that row at all and it was nothing that I had either done or not done, the coming home at the end of my work day daily row was a result of your mothers mental health and her having pent up all her rage all day with no one to take it out on, she had been waiting all day for me to get home so she could direct her rage towards me I came to realize that this behavior was a repetitive behavior that would never change and I could no longer accept it anymore and that was that!

I had tolerated this behavior now every day for the last two years this had become the normal daily pattern, silent treatment and full-on rage when we were face to face and hundreds of abusive vile insulting text messages all day while I was trying to work.

I had grown weary of your mother belittling me and insulting me all the time, she never missed the opportunity to hurt me and terrorize me whenever she could, I just accepted her insults now, I had become so numb with it all, I hurt so badly but I really couldn't possibly hurt any worse now, and the more I thought it all over in my mind the more I convinced myself that our situation would never improve, it would never get better and it would never go back to how things were when we first go together, I had to stop lying to myself that your mother would change, I knew in my heart that she wouldn't, the many times I had left your mother, then her broken promises of changing, she had no intention of changing herself, ever, your mother was far too lazy and stubborn to change, I could see this now, and I finally admitted to myself that I had given your mother too many chances to make positive changes over the last few years and she had chosen not to, so it was now down to me to make better lifestyle choices for myself, and I had been forced by your mother to cut her out of all the choices I knew I needed to make in my life now.

The insults and threats from your mother continued all through November, we didn't attend any friends' parties for Halloween, in fact we didn't go out together at all anymore, we were living totally separate lives under the same roof, and I had no intention of moving back into the spare room again, I wanted out of this toxic environment altogether now.

*I came to realize that things will only change
when I am brave enough to make the
necessary changes and not before.*

I had allowed your mother to terrorize my head, I was terrified of your mother, terrified of what she would do to me, she was bigger than me and so very aggressive towards me, I had lost so much weight I now weighed in at 6.5 stone that is 42 kilos, your mother was 19 stone that is 119 kilos, she was three times heavier than me, and I knew that if things ever got physical she could inflict some serious damage to me, she used to threaten to punch me and kick me and hurt me even though she only did this a few times, but my head had been held prisoner by the messages your mother used to send me, she used to make me feel so scared, but now I was starting to make so many connections in my head.

I had been living my life in constant fear of a personal attack being launched on me at any moment, but looking back now, your mother never actually followed through with any of her threats, she did shove me a few times but never laid a hand on me, I had come to realize it was all just words and empty threats, your mother had kept me living in constant fear of personal attacks that she knew she would never carry out but I didn't know that, I wasn't taking this anymore.

No one talks about men being abused, it seems to be the silent trauma, we are left to just deal with it, our friends and family look at us like we are crazy if we even try to mention anything regarding us being abused in any way at all, the expectation is that we can handle this being men and all, we are made to feel less than adequate if we can't handle the women in our lives, but when we get ourselves involved with dominant controlling women us normal men struggle to maintain control on the situation, I realized I never had the control on the situation, right from the start I was being lied to, gaslighted and manipulated by your mother, and now I knew that she would always be like this.

*Not every woman can be reasoned
with, and unfortunately Eliza your
mother is one of those women.*

Another scare tactic of your mothers was to just take off with no word to anyone of where she was going, she did this to me so many times this year that it lost its power over me, I started to lose concern for your mother and worry more about the potential damage she may do to my van that she always took off driving.

The first time your mother took off in my van with no word, she left me, your grandmother and your brother all terrified of what could have happened to her, your grandmother called the police who informed us that your mother was last spotted driving over to a friends' house, we all knew what your mother was doing at that friends' house, she was taking drugs and drinking, her phone was turned off so none of us could contact her, and we had no choice but to sit and wait for her to return home, when she did arrive back home she would smell of alcohol and be slurring her words and we were not allowed to question her on what she had been doing or who she had been with, if we dared to question your mother she became aggressive and abusive.

Last month in October when your mother had kicked me out of the flat again just so she could hold a drinks and drugs party that I wasn't allowed to be in the flat for was my breaking point I think, something inside me changed and all the while I was staying at my friends' house being advised by them to leave your mother, I just knew that I no longer wanted to live my life hanging around waiting for your mother to change, your mother was having fun with her friends at these parties she kept going to and holding at her flat, your mother was just so self-absorbed that she was oblivious to the fact that I was constantly being upset by her aggressive behavior and that I had finally made my mind up that I wasn't going to keep going back to her anymore, I had decided that this time when I left her I was never going back, no matter how hard she tried to make it for me or how much she promised to change, this toxic drama saga just had to stop, and I knew your mother was not capable of stopping any of it, so it had to be me that stopped it all and the only way I could do this was to leave and not come back!

> I couldn't live like this anymore; my mental health had reached a breaking point that I knew if I didn't leave, I would never recover from.

With all my love

Dad

CHAPTER NINETEEN

*Broken promises are likened
to broken records*

*December 1, 2021 T-Minus 9 months
before your due date.*

Dear Eliza,

The month of December was spent being bounced between silent treatment to full blown abusive outbursts suffered at the hands of your mother. My head was in a constant spin, I didn't know if I was coming or going, I couldn't think straight, I just wanted the ground to open and swallow me, I knew well in advance of the month of December even arriving that your mother would be extra abusive.

I saw all my friends and family preparing for Christmas, they were putting up their trees and decorations in their homes, they had begun their Christmas shopping and neatly wrapped presents were starting to appear underneath the trees, my social media was exploding with happy faces, crazy knitted Christmas jumpers being worn and lots of photos of peoples trees, I love to see photos of peoples trees, there is just something about them, every tree you see is different, different shapes and sizes, different color schemes, different lights on them, I was just loving seeing all of this on my feed.

> *But all these people had the one thing I
> didn't have................... Happiness.*

I just couldn't find it within myself to be happy I was incapable of feeling happy, I had the stuffing kicked out of me over the last few years and had reached a point in my life where I was sad every single day, I couldn't find one single happy thing to focus on, anything I tried to be happy about or show an interest in your mother would immediately smash it down.

Your mother would rob my happiness, she destroyed any chance of happiness I ever had or ever could have, any future with your mother was over for me, we had both reached a point where we just couldn't move forward with our lives, every single thing was catastrophic, even the smallest issues were blown out of proportion by your mother, we could no longer work together to find ways of coping with anything, it had been like this for a very long time now.

I hated being in the same room as your mother, I knew that she would turn her anger towards me with absolutely everything, every single little thing was my fault never hers, she was an expert at deflecting the blame onto me without taking any blame upon herself.

Our situation had become unfair and extremely toxic.

The week leading up to Christmas Day, your mother was quiet and sulking, we hardly spoke to each other now unless we were arguing over something your mother was blaming me for that I know I hadn't done! My head was twisted all over the place. What should have been a happy time with family and friends was an uncomfortable awful experience trapped in the flat with your mother that I will never forget for the rest of my life.

I really wanted my torture to end, I wanted to be with someone who appreciated my hard work, and loved me for who I am, I wanted a life partner who I could share my life with, someone who I could sit comfortably with, someone I could feel safe with, a person who I could relax with and trust them to not lie to me or attack me out of the blue with no reason, a person who was kind in their nature and would not falsely accuse me of the things I was not doing.

Your mother's perception of reality was so warped, she had tainted my perception of things too, I knew that I had to work hard at repairing myself, moving closer towards a better life for myself, I knew I would never be allowed to do this with your mother, I needed to get away from here so I could start to heal.

I knew that the kind of life I wanted wouldn't just happen, I knew I had to make this happen, it was time to forge the life that I wanted for myself, time to stop tolerating bad behavior from your mother, time to let go and start again, and that time was now.

With all my love

Dad

CHAPTER TWENTY

The Great Escape

December 25, 2021 - Christmas Day – T-Minus 9 months before your due date.

Dear Eliza,

Well, what can I say, now I have made my decision that I need to leave this toxic situation with your mother. This day was spent over at your grandmother's house, we were having Christmas dinner, I was sitting with your brother in the front room while your mother and grandmother made dinner in the kitchen.

My mind was racing, trying to think of ways to leave your mother for good, I was trying to think of a way of leaving that would be acceptable to your mother, a way that she would accept and not terrorize me into returning like she had done several times before in the past.

I was trying to think of where I could live, somewhere safe, a place that your mother couldn't find me and terrorize me at, I had to escape from her controlling clutches, and wherever I moved to I had to be safe and out of your mother's clutches. I knew that if your mother knew where I was living that she would come and terrify me at that address, and I knew she would never leave me alone to get on with repairing my life.

I was alone in my thoughts, as I sat in the front room, I could hear your mother and grandmother talking together, there was no happiness in the kitchen and no laughter, just low voices, when we were called to the table your brother and me got up and moved into the dining room. We all sat together at the table as dinner had been served and your mother boldly announced she was pregnant!

I almost choked! Your mother had announced your presence like this intentionally to force yet another reaction out of me in front of her family.

Your mother was deathly silent, and your grandmother said to me "So what are you going to do about the baby then?" and my reply was "I will support the baby" your mother hardly spoke to me after that, we only spoke to each other when we had to, and all conversations between us were forced and quickly ended now. I didn't know what to say, all my thoughts about leaving your mother were halted, I now had something else that I needed to think about, and that something was you.

I didn't know what to do, I had made my decision to leave, and I was adamant that I had to leave, I couldn't go back on my plans now, I had taken all I could this year and I knew that having a baby thrown into the mix now would make things ten times worse. I had to carry on with my plan to leave, I couldn't stay with your mother any longer, I still intended to leave.

I couldn't stay at the flat, I no longer felt comfortable there, I had never felt at home at the flat, the flat was given to your mother by the council to house her and your brother, it wasn't my home, it had never felt like home to me, it was your mothers' place, so I had to leave and build a home for myself away from here.

All my love

Dad

CHAPTER TWENTY-ONE

December 31, 2021 - New Years Eve – T-Minus 9 months before your due date.

Dear Eliza,

All my family had arranged to go to a New Years Eve party at the local pub, they invited me to go with them all, but I really didn't feel like going out and being in a large crowd of people, I now found that I didn't feel comfortable in social settings anymore, and even though it was my family asking me to go out with them, and I had promised myself last year that this year would be so different, I still found that I didn't want to go, I just didn't feel safe in public places anymore, I had a new feeling of heightened anxiety that I just couldn't seem to shift, all the promises I had made to myself last year had all gone up in smoke now.

I spent the evening at the flat, sitting in silence back in the spare room AGAIN thoughts racing through my mind.

I was upset and feeling overwhelmed with thoughts of failure, not knowing how I was even going to start my recovery when I wasn't even close to having a plan. All I knew at this moment in time was that I needed to work out a way of leaving so both your mother and me could begin to recover and I was angry at your mother for disclosing that she was pregnant in front of your grandmother and your brother without telling me first.

But that was your mother all over, only ever considered her own feelings and never the feelings of others, and especially not me, I felt she had engineered that little revelation ceremony to maximize the hurt inflicted on me, to announce that kind of thing in front of your mothers' family without me knowing beforehand was another tactic of your mothers inflicted on me, to rub it in my face that everyone else was way more important than me, and that everyone else knew except for me, I felt embarrassed that all eyes were on me when your mother announced she was going to have a baby and that I didn't know but everyone else sitting around the table did.

She had intentionally left me out, I know that your grandmother had known of the pregnancy way before I did, your grandmother didn't even react when your mother announced she was expecting you and neither did your brother. I am your father, and yet I was the last to know of your existence, I should have been the second to know once your mother found out.

I don't want to live with a person who treats me so cruelly, I just don't!

I'm still going ahead with leaving.

All my love

Dad

CHAPTER TWENTY-TWO

I'm Free

January 1, 2022 – Day 1 of my departure T-Minus 8 months before your due date.

Dear Eliza,

I managed to find somewhere I could stay; I packed my van with all my belongings, and I left.

The relief I felt was amazing, I had found a means to escape, so I took it, I had been given a lifeline of hope, this was going to be the start of my new life, a chance to rebuild myself and make plans going forward, my plan to build somewhere that we can both be safe, somewhere that I can live and you can visit, somewhere peaceful and calm where we could both sit in safety away from your mothers dramas and screaming fits.

All of a sudden I could see a brighter future for myself, I could start the healing process and rebuild my mental health, I could start to recover financially as your mother had taken a lot of my money for her own needs and this had left me rather short on finances, I could just about make the rent I had to pay at my new location, but it was a start for me, and a start that I desperately needed to make too.

My newly found freedom didn't last long before I started to receive messages from your mother, she was demanding to know where I was so she could come over, she assumed I had moved back to my parents' house, so I allowed her to think this. It was safer for me if she thought she knew where I was, because I knew that she would stop at nothing to find me otherwise!

MY parents were sworn to secrecy to protect me from your mother discovering my whereabouts, my whole family had been informed of our toxic relationship and how I needed to be protected from your mother lashing out at me with her rage attacks.

I had agreed with my parents to park my van outside their house overnight so it looked like I was living there, I knew your mother would be driving past late at night and in the early hours of the morning to check my van hadn't moved.

I told my closest friends of my predicament, as your mother started to message them all asking for information on what I was doing and where I was going, she tried to manipulate me into going back to her at the flat, a tactic she had used on me many times in the past, a tactic using emotional blackmail, playing on my weak emotions, trying to make me feel sorry for her, when these subtle tactics didn't work on me anymore she became extremely angry and abusive towards me, and when she knew she could no longer control me this way she began using a more sinister approach trying to manipulate me into doing exactly what she wanted me to do, she would threaten to hurt herself or kill herself and you growing inside her, putting the blame on me for her and you dying because I wouldn't do what she wanted me to do.

I was still living in a state of sheer terror, terrified that your mother would kill herself and you too, I hadn't managed to escape your mothers' control at all, I was still living in fear of what she would do next.

Your mother had threatened to kill herself many times over the time we were together, she had never tried to kill herself, but she knew the terror of her words would play on my emotions and it always led to me giving into her and going back to the relationship and now she had you to weaponize against me too, your mother was only three weeks pregnant with you when the threats to kill you started for me, your mother knew she had yet another thing to weaponize against me now.

Your mother had a new way of trying to coerce me into doing what she wanted me to do, but I knew nothing would change, I knew that if I did give in and do what your mother wanted me to do that the negativity would remain the same, along with the emotional blackmail and the daily arguments, so too did the put downs and control tactics, every day would be spent being controlled and dominated by your mother, I couldn't move without her knowing about it, I couldn't spend time with family or friends, your mother would just go right back to ringing me every time I visited my mother, calls that consisted of your mother insulting me AND my mother, accusing me of being a baby and running back to my mother to protect me, calling me a coward and being weak for not standing up for myself, but if I did attempt to stand up for myself I was accused of bullying, I had to stay strong now more than ever, a baby was coming and I had to find the strength to heal myself and prepare myself for your arrival.

Even though I had moved out today, I was still not free from your mother's terrifying tortuous methods of control. I was in the middle of a no-win situation of constant abuse, with me being wrong with every single situation that unfolded. I was monitored, my vehicle was monitored, my phone was monitored, I felt like I was suffocating like I couldn't breathe.

I shouldn't be feeling like this now I no longer live with your mother.

But above all else, no matter what happens or what your mother tries to threaten me with I know I have to remain strong and not crumble like I have done in the past, I cannot go back to your mother, I know that she would make my life a living hell all over again, and I know that I would be used and abused as I have been for a few years now.

If I go back now, all my efforts will be for nothing, and I know that once you are born that I would be used by your mother as a slave to get everything done in the flat and to take care of you too, your mother will run me into the ground.

I just can't go back Eliza, I just can't.

All my love

Dad

CHAPTER TWENTY-THREE

I am not free!

*January 2, 2022 – Day 2 of my departure T-
Minus 8 months before your due date.*

Dear Eliza,

The day started off with hundreds of messages from your mother ranting about how awful a person I am, how disgusting I am, how vile I am, what a failure I am, I received message after message of narcissistic rage solely directed at me, your mother was forcefully telling me using the most awful derogatory language possible to describe how she felt about me, and in the same sentence asking me if I am coming home?

The whirlwind of abuse I received was unbelievable, when I showed your mothers messages to my family they could not believe what they were reading, they were shocked at the content of the messages and they were shocked at the speed at which these messages were being delivered too, your mother just didn't stop, I received message after message, I was verbally insulted and attacked if I didn't reply back to your mother instantly, and I was struggling to keep up with her messages, before I could finish reading one message I had received another 5 more!

I wanted to talk about you, and what should have been a happy occasion was taken away from me AGAIN.

The way the news of your existence was revealed to me at Christmas sitting at the table with your mothers' family all looking at me asking me what I am going to do now, boom! I have a child! Just like that, I am going to be a father, I had no adjustment time, no time to allow the news to sink in gently, just announced out of the blue, putting me on the spot, then the uncomfortable silence forced on me by your mother when we left the house to go back to the flat was unbearable too.

Thankfully your brother was living at your grandmothers at the time because your mother didn't want him at the flat, she wanted to enjoy not having the responsibility of having to look after a child, so she had sent him to live at your grandmothers a few years beforehand, of course this will never be the story she tells you about why your brother never lived with you until I left, somehow this will be turned around to be my fault again, I will get the blame for not wanting him at the flat or something!

Every joyous occasion in my life has always been soured by your mother's jealousy, every potentially happy moment taken from me, tainted and downplayed, always leaving me with a deflated outlook on things.

And now I am separated from you, and I just know this will be played out as my fault entirely with no blame ever having been apportioned to your mother, your mother will do the same to you that she did to your brother. Your mother wouldn't allow your brother to see his father until he was about eight years old, this ensured she had enough time to successfully poison him against his father ensuring that he held a low opinion of the man and making him not want to see him at all, and I just knew this would happen to me too.

I'm in bits.

All my love

Dad

CHAPTER TWENTY-FOUR

January 12, 2022 Proof of Life Test T-Minus 8 months before your due date.

Dear Eliza,

After days of receiving hateful messages from your mother, she sent me a photo today of a pregnancy test she performed, she thought that I would think she was lying about being pregnant with you, so she did a test and sent me proof, that I never asked for!

Your mother asked me if I wanted to come to the scans, and I was happy to be asked, of course I wanted to come to the scans, of course I wanted to be involved in everything to do with my own child.

But then, the emotional blackmail started, the moment your mother had another bargaining tool, she began to message using being a part of your life as something I had to earn, I had to do everything your mother said I had to do just to gain a few minutes to you.

Your mother was demanding that I go back to her, and that would be the only way I would ever get to see you or be a part of your life, your mothers expectations of being a family were to be adhered to at all times, and if I didn't play along to her demands, I was callously kicked to the curb for daring to have an opinion of my own.

All through January your mother tried to get me to move back in with her, she told me she couldn't cope, she told me I couldn't go to any of your scans if I didn't do what she wanted me to do, your mother was constantly using you as a weapon against me, your mother had always made me chose things in our relationship, she would accuse me of loving something more than her and your mother would make me chose her over whatever it was that

I wanted to do, your mother would emotionally blackmail me by saying things like "if you loved me, you would want to do that" and "if you loved me, you wouldn't go there" your mother did this all the time when I went to motocross events, she would start messaging me saying that I loved motocross more than her, and that if I truly loved her I wouldn't go, I would give it all up for her, I had to constantly prove my love for your mother by sacrificing the things I loved, and now it was your turn to be used against me.

Your mother started saying things like "I don't want to raise my child alone, she needs a father, I grew up without one and it isn't nice" then she would say "if you loved this baby you would come back and be a family" truth is we were never a family, your brother was sent to live with your grandmother and your mother was incapable of looking after children, your mother wanted me to do all the hard work and I knew what her plan was, I would be bullied into doing everything while your mother sat back and told everyone how fantastic she was and how awful I was. I didn't want to set myself up like this, I had a plan that I would take you away from that toxic situation and get to spend time with you in a mentally healthier environment with my family and friends instead of you getting to see me being abused at the flat by your mother.

Your mother started a smear campaign on me, she told her friends and family that I just walked out on her when she told me she was pregnant, which was a lie, your mother failed to inform them that she had been emotionally attacking me for two years leading up to me leaving the relationship, that bit of her tale seemed to be left out entirely, yet again, making me out to be such an awful man for leaving "his pregnant girlfriend just after Christmas" oh what a cu@t I am!

I didn't bother to defend myself at all, because I know everyone would believe your mother because she tells a fantastic story about how bad I am, there really is no point in even trying to stand up for myself at all, your mother had been bad mouthing me for years without any resistance from me, so I knew the people your mother was speaking to had already been brain

73

washed and conditioned by your mother to accept me as the bad guy in everything.

So, I let it all go, I never retaliate to her lies about me, I didn't defend myself and I just let people believe what they want to believe about me, I am way past the point of caring what other people think of me anymore and your mother holds such a low opinion of me that there really is no repairing that at all................ EVER!

All my love

Dad

CHAPTER TWENTY-FIVE

February 25, 2022 – Your First Scan Date T-
Minus 7 months before your due date.

Dear Eliza,

Following on from the abuse I received from your mother the whole of January, she finally messaged me and asked me if I wanted to come to your scan, I accepted the invitation.

I arranged to pick your mother up so we could go to the hospital together as I felt this was the right thing to do, however, the moment your mother got in my van, she started to verbally attack me, asking me why I had left and why I wasn't going back to live with her, she told me she had seen my van parked at my parents' house and demanded that I go back to the flat with her.

I tried to tell her the relationship between us was over, I didn't want to go back to her and live in such a toxic environment, I tried to explain that I had every right to leave a situation that I was not happy being in, this just infuriated your mother even more, because this is not what she wanted to hear, she became violently angry with me and we argued the whole way to your scan appointment.

Once your mother was in front of witnesses in a public place the abuse stopped, as I knew it would, but I also knew it was only temporary, as going from past experiences of your mother's rage attacks, I knew the moment we were back in the van out of earshot of other people that the verbal attacks would resume where she had left off.

While we were in the hospital, I got to see you on the screen, sitting in the dark room watching the sonographer moving the wand back and forth across your mother's tummy, I got to see your head, your little hands and feet, you were all curled up in a ball, and I felt love for you immediately.

It was strange seeing you for the first time, knowing you were inside your mother, and I was truly happy at that time.

That happiness was short lived, as the moment the appointment was over and we were heading back to drop your mother off, it all started again, the abuse, the horrible treatment, the vindictive words your mother used to put me down, to upset me and paralyze me with fear.

I couldn't wait until your mother was out of my van, I couldn't wait to get back to the safety of my new home, somewhere I felt totally safe, a place where your mother couldn't get to me, and I was safely out of her reach, when I parked up I got out the van and practically ran down the path to my safe space.

The rest of February was spent arguing by messages with your mother, being called the most horrid names, being terrified of her vile threats, your mother using you as a bargaining tool to control me and manipulate me into doing exactly what she wanted me to do for her.

She uninvited me to the rest of the scan dates, she told me I wasn't welcome to come and that I would not be present at your birth either, your mother told me she would let me know once you were born and maybe allow me to see you then, your mother told me that she was going to block me and not speak to me until after you were born at which point she would contact me then.

Just as I had predicted, your mother has ensured that I don't have anything to do with her pregnancy and nothing to do with you at all, I will have to wait until you are born now to have any form of contact with you at all.

Again, your mother is saying this to make sure she inflicts maximum pain on me, your mother keeps saying that if I go back to live with her though, then and ONLY then can I play a part in your life, but if I keep choosing to be a "little cu@t about things, then I can fu@k off and die" and "that I will NEVER see you"

My heart is breaking with all the threats by your mother, why can't she just be normal, why can't she just be reasonable? Why does every interaction between us have to be so venomous and horrendous? Why is your mother so abusive and nasty to me all the time? She needs specialist help; she has deep-rooted unresolved childhood traumas that are seriously affecting her interactions with me.

I am not the one to blame for anything bad that happened to your mother in her life before she met me and yet I am punished every day for them.

I don't know how I am going to get through the next few months before you are born, I am trying to tell myself that all of this is out of my control, there is nothing I can do I am powerless yet again, but there is one certainty now, you are here and you are arriving soon whether your mother likes it or not, there is a time limit on how long she can use you to threaten me with.

All my love

Dad

CHAPTER TWENTY-SIX

Hell, hath no fury like your mother

*March, 2022 – Hell via Messenger T-minus
6 months before your due date.*

Dear Eliza,

All the month of March was spent with your mother sending the vilest of messages to me after she said she was going to block me until you were born, but as usual your mother blocked me for a few days, then unblocked me when she wanted to start abusing me again.

Your mother was calling me all the names under the sun, threatening to kill herself and you, instantly blocking me after sending these vile messages so I couldn't reply, then deleting her messages after sending, then unblocking me, your mother was an absolute nightmare, she had my head spinning.

I tried to approach your grandmother to attempt to get her to talk to your mother to reason with her and calm her down, I wanted to be involved in your life, I wanted to be a part of raising you, but your mother would not allow me to do this and once she discovered I had approached your grandmother she just became even more abusive towards me, saying I was weak and a coward because I wouldn't talk directly to your mother about things, but she was making every bit of communication impossible.

Your mother pushed me out of everything that involved you, the only time your mother was civil to me was when she was asking me to buy you things that you needed, your mother would send me links to websites showing me what prams she wanted and what nursery furniture she wanted for you, then after your mother sent these links I would ask her if she wanted me to buy it she verbally attacked me saying she doesn't want anything from me and she is more than capable of getting everything she needs for you herself!

I have no idea what to say to your mother anymore, nothing I say or do is ever good enough for her, so I am going to stop trying.

All my love

Dad

CHAPTER TWENTY-SEVEN

March 24, 2022 your mother sent me pictures
of your second scan, you are getting bigger now
– T-Minus 6 months before your due date.

Dear Eliza,

The remainder of this month has been spent trying to reason with your mother, she blows hot and cold, she is erratic and totally unpredictable, I really cannot keep up with her mood swings, I try to be non-committal with everything I say, as it doesn't matter what I say or how I say it, your mother gets triggered into reacting with extreme outbursts of venomous rage.

I am constantly treading on eggshells trying so hard not to trigger your mother, but I fail so miserably, my family are telling me to find someone impartial to act as a mediator in between the two of us, my mother thinks the relationship has totally broken down between us now and that if this carries on like this there will never be any chance of having a positive connection between us in the future.

There needs to be good communication so we are able to talk maturely about arrangements for your upbringing when you are born, but I don't think your mother is able to do this at all, she behaved exactly the same towards your brothers father too and I just knew she would behave this way with me as well, she is just nasty and vile with her attitude towards me, she hates me for everything, there isn't a day that goes by that I don't get the blame for something or other, I am made to feel terrible every single day, your mothers says that I should be made to feel bad as I don't deserve happiness in my life, because your mother blames me for ruining her life.

All the time we were together, not once did I ever retaliate towards your mother, not once did I call her hurtful names, I was NEVER malicious towards her, if I didn't have anything nice to say back to your mother all the time I was receiving abuse I just didn't say anything to her at all, but even when I adopted the polite or the politely quiet approach I still received abuse, your mother would insult me by calling me a pussy and accusing me of being weak because I wouldn't fight with her, but I don't want to fight with her, I wanted to hold normal conversations about normal everyday things, but your mother always turns everything into a massive drama and a fight that she HAS to win.

I am tolerating her abuse just so I can remain connected with your mother, being connected with her keeps me connected with you, I am hoping that her rage will just subside, and a more normal version of your mother will magically appear one day.

All my love

Dad

CHAPTER TWENTY-EIGHT

*April 28, 2021 – We found out you are a little
girl T-minus 5 months before your due date.*

Dear Eliza,

I have tried so hard to reason with your mother, I tried asking what bits your mother needed and I offered to buy them for you, but your mother rejects everything I say, she accuses me of not caring about her or you, but I do care, I care very much, your mother always tells me how I feel, she tries to tell me that I am not upset or hurt by her rantings, she has no idea how I feel, all she does is project her insecurities and fears onto me, she tries to make her failures mine, just because your mother cannot find happiness in anything she doesn't want me to find it either!

She informed me that she has been referred to social services due to her mental health, and to be honest I am relieved, maybe now she will receive expert help that she so desperately needs, I am happy that at last someone has picked up on her mental health, but she then tells me that the reason she has been referred to the mental health team is because she told them that I make her feel so bad.

Your mother told the mental health team that I make her have suicidal thoughts about killing herself and you, and that I am to blame for the way she is, another lie, and the mental health team have believed every word she fed them too!

Your mother was suicidal before we got together, there are posts on her social media from years before we got together saying she wanted to end things for herself and your brother, and that she couldn't see a way forward with her life and your brothers, now she was saying the same things to me about you, your mother told me she had reported me to the mental health team and had given them all my details including my home address at my parents' house, your mother told me that if anything happens to either her or you that I would be blamed for it, another fear tactic.

This is what your mother is telling me, but I have no idea whether or not it is true or made up, your mother spins such great lies, I never know when she is lying to me or telling the truth, I suppose there must be an element of truth in there somewhere that she has been referred to the mental health team but the facts have been manipulated to make out that your mother is the victim in all of this, deflecting the blame for her behavior onto others yet again!

Your mother fails to tell anyone that she is still hanging onto the past, it is mentally unhealthy for her to do this, she is not thinking about the effect she is having on everyone else around her, only herself, everything is always about your mother and what she wants and how she feels, she controls every situation, she micromanages me and everything else, and I can't cope with being micromanaged by her any longer, your mother never tells the truth when it comes to how bad her life is, she is exactly where she chose to put herself, no one else made her do any of the things she does, and no one has ever made her say the abusive vile things she says, that all comes from her, she is incapable of taking any blame for herself, all she ever does is blame everyone else for the way she is.

I am trying to move forward in my life, but your mother makes it very difficult, because she is unable to move forward herself, she doesn't want me to. She attempts to drag me back into her toxic world using every tactic she knows of constantly deflecting all the blame onto me, so she never takes any responsibility for anything herself.

I cannot make your mother see that I no longer want to be in a relationship with her, but I do want to be actively involved in your life with you, I cannot get your mother to see that we would be better raising you together as friends, living separately where you get to see the best of both of us, spending your time between us both, seeing the happier side of us both, but your mother is insisting on raising you together in a toxic environment full of arguments and abuse. This is not what I want for you or myself, but my feelings are not even being considered here at all, everything is being looked at from your mother's point of view as it always is.

Your mother keeps saying to me that she wants to raise you together with me living back at the flat, that she doesn't want you to grow up without a father, your mother keeps telling me that she had to grow up without a father as her mother and father had split up when she was very young, and then her father died, but I had no control over any of that, and I feel that your mother has this unhinged view of how the perfect family should be, she carries feelings of failure after her relationship with your brothers father failed, the story that your mother tells here is that your brothers father cheated on her, and she didn't do anything wrong to make the relationship end, she is mirroring that story now with our relationship ending, I know for sure how our relationship ended and it wasn't with me cheating or lying to your mother, so now I question everything about what your mother has told me regarding your brothers father and that breakup? If what your mother is saying about me is untrue then there must also be lies being told regarding her previous partner too???

A leopard never changes its spots, I know that break ups are hard to handle, and I understand that it is easier to get angry at the other person for leaving, but to lie to other people and to yourself about why the relationship ended is just not helping in your recovery at all.

Your mother keeps sending me links to articles that say a baby needs their father, but they need a safe father who can be relied on and depended on, I am honest, hardworking, reliable and dependable, but your mother is the one preventing me from getting involved all because I won't give in to what she wants and go back to living with her, I will never see you at this rate, as I am not giving in to your mother and going back to her, I have to make a stand not only for myself but for you too.

I don't want to be abused by your mother in front of you, I

don't want to live in an unhealthy environment where you get to witness your mother abusing me and treating me like dirt every day, that is what you will learn to do to me too, and I don't want that for myself, I can't go back to your mother………….. EVER!

Your mother was given a due date of 7th September 2022, but your mother will be induced three weeks earlier on 15th August due to all your mothers' health conditions, which she has also blamed me for, her being 119kilos, my fault, her having gestational diabetes, my fault, her having Obstetric Biliary Cirrhosis, my fault, her unhealthy lifestyle with no exercise, my fault, her bad eating habits, my fault, her constant urine infections, my fault, my fault, my fault, my fault, my fault, my fault, bloody everything is my faulty, Jesus Christ take some blame on yourself woman.

Your due date seems so far away right now, but I know the time will pass quickly from now until then, I am excited about the prospect of your arrival, but I just know your mother will make absolutely everything to do with you difficult, and I already know that she won't make things easy for me where you are concerned and this will be forever, not just when you are first born, I know damn well this will be every single communication between us for the entirety of your life and mine!

I think I have always known that your mother would never make any dealings between us easy for me, and I have come to expect the nastiness of your mother to be directed at me all the time.

All my love

Dad

CHAPTER TWENTY-NINE

Is it me or is there another issue here?

*May, 2022 - Getting nowhere fast T-minus
4 months before your due date.*

Dear Eliza,

This month's messages are fliting between your mother asking me why I left her and just abusing me, we have been over this so many times I have lost count, she refuses to accept the truthful reason I left, and that I left because of how she treated me, because she is not hearing what she wants to hear, she is asking the same questions over and over again, this is her way of rewriting the true version of events, she keeps asking and asking until I give in to her version of what happened, she beats me into submission so she can say anything she likes I have always given into her in the past I found it easier to just agree and get the punishment over with faster.

But not this time, that happened in the past, that is not happening now and your mother really does not like the way I am stronger now, she doesn't like how I stand up for myself better now, she hates how strong I am becoming, and she has tried to change tactics, she is softer in the way she is speaking to me, trying to coerce me into saying what she wants me to say.

Your mother will not accept the truth of why I left her, she can't handle the truth, she lies to herself and anyone who will listen to her, she convinces others that I am the cause of her mental health issues and that I am to blame for her behavior, even though she is an adult and responsible for her own behavior, but there is always an excuse as to why she said awful things to me and why she did horrible things to me.

Your mother would always say either I made her do it, or I made her feel angry, or that she was having a bad day and that was all the justification she needed to verbally attack me. I was in such a miserable state that I didn't know whether I was coming or going, my mind was in total confusion following our arguments, being accused of things I hadn't said or done, it left me feeling like I didn't know who I was anymore my sense of reality being distorted, and her version of events being taken as the truth, your mother just had to be right in every situation she had to win every confrontation, even if it meant me losing my mind over it all, your mother didn't care about me.

One tiny little thing would set your mother off into an abusive rage, she had isolated me from friends and family, I had been intentionally cut off from my support network to help me and I found I had no one to turn to for assistance, I knew deep down inside that things were wrong, but I had no idea how to fix them.

I met someone, someone really nice who I could sit and talk to, she made me feel very relaxed in her company, and she had the same interests as I did too, she rode fast motorbikes and had a camper van that she went trekking with, she enjoys the great outdoors and she is very active, her hobbies include, hiking, mountain biking, reading and she runs her own photography business, she is the total opposite of your mother, this lady is positive and has a great sense of adventure about her, I knew that your mother would not take the news very well, I thought that after our relationship being so tumultuous over the last 2 years and me leaving over 5 months ago that we would have managed to work out our differences by now and that we would be talking on a friendship basis, but your mother was being so horrible about the whole thing, she was refusing to acknowledge that there were issues long before I left and that those issues caused me to leave, and also, that those issues were not resolving, we were not able to address the problems in our relationship because your mother was in denial of there being any issues, she refused to see that her behavior was not acceptable, and she thought that I would just continue to put up with being abused and humiliated by her without making a stand for myself.

I was never able to mention anything about seeing anyone else to your mother while messaging, because she had not reached a point where she had accepted our breakup as final, your mother still had it in her head that I would eventually be talked into going back to her like I had done several times before over the past 2 years.

I knew how aggressive your mother could be, and I also knew that your mother would cause a lot of trouble for me and my new girlfriend is she ever found out. It wouldn't have mattered how long we had been apart for either, even if we had been separated for a few years, I knew your mother would never accept me being with anyone else except for her.

Your mother never reached a point where I could tell her that I was seeing someone else, I was still trying to convince your mother at this point that I was never going back and that our relationship had run its course and was over, I wanted to remain friends and raise you together, but your mother just was not going to let that happen…. EVER.

I knew your mother would make me out to be the bad guy to everyone yet again, but when I left your mother, I started to live my life my way, not the way I had been made to live by your mother, the day I left I broke free from her controlling hand and I was determined that I was never going back to her, no matter what she threatened me with, and I was no longer going to be forced to make choices over the things that I loved to do.

I told my new girlfriend about your mother, and I tried to explain how the relationship had become so toxic. My girlfriend could see all the messages I was constantly getting from your mother, she had suggested trying to come to some kind of mutual agreement and settle the air before you were born, she said that if we had not managed to clear the air before your birth that it would be so much harder to attempt to make any access arrangements if your mother and me were not on speaking terms, I knew this too, but my girlfriend and my family had no idea of how unreasonable your mother could be, and how futile my attempts at reasoning with your mother were.

Your mother is not a normal person, you cannot negotiate

anything normally with her, there is no common ground to stand on and my point of view or anyone else's point of view would ever be considered or respected by your mother, she knows best.

I had spent from January up until May just trying to get your mother to be civil towards me, something she just couldn't ever manage to do, no matter what approach I tried with your mother, there was just no reasoning with her, on any subject about anything at all, every single interaction with your mother was specifically engineered into a confrontation, every piece of information twisted into words of hatred, and every single suggested solution thrown back at me.

I knew I wasn't getting any further forward at all; I knew your mother would always make everything so much more complicated than it ever needed to be. I had come to accept that this is just how she is, and she will NEVER be any different to this.

Your mother had already banned me from further scans, she told me I wasn't welcome at the hospital, I would not be called in when your mother was giving birth and that I was not going to be involved in your life at all, your mother told me she was going to raise you on her own and that she was not going to let me be there for anything in your life.

Your mother told me that she had raised your brother on her own, even though she never needed to, and that she would do it again with you, even though I spent that last five months saying I wanted to be a part of your life and that I would care for you and provide for you too, but everything I said got flung back at me, there was just no getting through to your mother at all.

I didn't know how to respond to this.

All my love

Dad

CHAPTER THIRTY

I am getting nowhere fast!

June, 2022 – T-Minus 3 months before your due date.

Dear Eliza,

Your mother has been sending me pictures of our life together, pictures of you and the dogs, she has been sending me pictures of baby outfits and asking me again why I left her, she refuses to believe that the relationship is over for good and that I am not going back to her.

I just can't keep going over the same conversations, I am wasting my time explaining myself when she will never accept what I am saying to her, and as an adult I don't have to explain myself to your mother, our relationship ended months ago. The only thing we have linking us together now is you, and she is refusing to let me have anything to do with you, this is her way of punishing me and using you to torture me, weaponizing you against me every way she can, constantly threatening me saying, she will hurt herself, or she will hurt you, or I will never see you, she has thrown every single threat she can at me, I'm exhausted just listening to it all.

One minute your mother is telling me to fu@k off and never speak to her again, and the next message I receive is her asking me to go over and keep her company because she is lonely and bored, she uses me to suit her own desires, I am just a puppet she uses to play with when she is bored.

When I won't do as she is asking, she becomes verbally abusive, then deletes her abusive messages straight after sending them so I don't get chance to read any of them, then blocks me so I can't reply or stand up for myself, then she unblocks me and sends more abusive messages, then blocks me again!

This childish behavior is normal with your mother, and I am just expected to tolerate it all without saying anything.

My emotions are spent, my nerves are in tatters, and I can no longer cope with the constant yoyoing back and forth as your mother blows hot and cold on me, exacting her revenge on me for daring to want a better life for myself and leaving her.

Your mother has started saying about raising you together, but not living together, but she wants me to live back in the spare room at the flat, I just cannot go back to living with your mother, I know that your mother would go back to being able to abuse me, she wants me under her roof under her total control so she can say whatever she likes to me without anyone else hearing what she is saying, and she wants to be able to treat me like dirt without witnesses, I cannot get your mother to see that I am never going back to that kind of life ever again, I worked hard to get free from your mother, why on earth would I want to go back to that?

June 11, 2022 – the day your mother discovered I had a girlfriend T-Minus 3 months before your due date.

After arranging to meet up with your mother face to face as I needed a foot pump back, we met at my garage and she saw my engagement ring on my finger, needless to say she wasn't happy about it and immediately launched into a verbal assault on me, I had tried so many times to try to tell your mother that I had met someone else and that I wasn't coming back to her, but she just wouldn't accept anything I had to say, so over time I just stopped trying to say anything at all.

Your brother was in the car with her and heard everything she said to me, I just couldn't face hearing her going on about what a cun@t I was, I started to walk away, your mother drove off at speed.

121 messages of pure venom from your mother, the vindictiveness that I always feared began that day, timing wasn't great I know that, I had been trying to calm the situation

between your mother and me for months, but everything I suggested your mother didn't want to go along with, she insisted on presenting the most impossible scenarios that were doomed to failure due to setting unrealistic expectations from the start, she tried to manipulate and dictate absolutely everything, her need to control everything had driven us further apart, I knew she never had any intention of ever allowing me to see you, and yet despite this I still tried to reason with her, I was trying to protect myself from your mother and you also.

Yet again I failed at trying to protect us, but then again with you being inside your mother how could I ever protect you? And trying to protect myself was proving to be difficult enough.

All my love

Dad

CHAPTER THIRTY-ONE

*June 14, 2022 – I just had to block your
mother for my own sanity.*

Dear Eliza,

I reached a point today where I accepted that your mother had no intention of trying to move our situation forward in any way at all, I knew she had been playing cruel mind games with me all along, this was her way of punishing me for leaving her, I knew that she was always going to cause a massive drama with everything she ever did, and now she had you to throw into the mix too, this nightmare would never end for me and after enduring days of her hateful nature once again, I was left with no choice but to block her.

Your mother is delusional, creating fantasies in her mind of how she thinks her situation is, rather than looking at her situation factually, she refuses to accept our relationship has been over for months and that I have moved on with my life, I have made numerous promises to be there for you Eliza but I just cannot be there for your mother, she has broken me, she continues to break me, and she will work her hardest to keep me broken, she doesn't want me to repair myself because she is broken and she will never repair herself, she takes comfort in keeping me broken along with her.

After I blocked your mother, she started messaging my family and friends asking about what I am doing and who my new girlfriend is, she asked my friends to find out and tell her my girlfriend's name.

It wasn't long before someone disclosed my girlfriend's identity to your mother, and she immediately started to gather information on her, your mother removed pictures of my girlfriend off her social media and emailed them to me abusing me, as she couldn't text the pictures because I had blocked her.

June 16, 2022, I had to unblock your mother – T-Minus 3 months before your due date.

Your mother was causing such a nuisance of herself to my family and friends that I had to unblock your mother, I was embarrassed by her behavior, and I felt like I owed everyone an explanation as to why your mother was doing this, it wasn't long before your mother's abusive messages started again.

I was back to trying to reason with your mother AGAIN, she was demanding to know why I had left her AGAIN, she wasn't moving the conversation forward at all, we were still going over the same issues that we were arguing about in January, and here we are in June some months later with your mother demanding answers to the same questions she has been asking me for months, and I was still giving the same answers that she didn't want to hear but were the truth, I had no other answers to give!

I asked your mother to stop asking the same questions, I pleaded with her to accept things are over between us, that I would still be there to support you Eliza, but your mother was totally unreasonable as usual and nothing I said was being acknowledged, your mother made every argument about her, her thoughts, her feelings, her needs, her wants, her, her, her, and her, no one else ever being considered at all.

Every time I tried to point out that your mother was being unreasonable and that she was being abusive towards me, she immediately excused her behavior towards me as justified because she was angry, or that she felt upset, or that she was having a bad day, or that I deserved to be spoken to like I didn't matter, but there was always an excuse for her to blame her behavior on, the pattern that had emerged a few years ago way before this day arrived was still very much present today too.

Our conversations just going round in never ending circles, never resolving any of our personal issues, constant upset and trauma, ongoing drama sagas that just went on and on from one day to the next, continuing into the next day, week, month and year with no progress being made, I was told by my family to just move on, they all advised me that this should have changed by now, my family were all worried about me, they could see I was near to breaking with it all and had been all year.

After receiving hundreds of messages from your mother in one day, I blocked her again.

I left it a day and unblocked your mother on Friday 17 June, 2022.

Instantly my phone started pinging with messages being sent by your mother, I started to read through all the messages hitting my phone, messages of hatred and nastiness filling my inbox, accusing me of cheating on your mother when I never cheated on her, the conversation taking its usual direction towards blaming me for everything that goes wrong, the emotional blackmail tactics, the guilt trips being put on me, saying you Eliza will suffer now because of me, you don't get a father in your life, even though your mother could have included me but she was the one making all the choices and your mother was the one who held all the control over everything, as all women do in domestic abuse cases against men.

Men have no control, no rights over anything, social stigma dictates that we are men and should be able to handle these kinds of situations, but the failure here is, no one seems to understand the difficulties men have trying to deal with unreasonable women who hold all the cards in the relationship.

The steady destruction of our emotional wellbeing, the decline in our mental health, the long-term systematic bullying inflicted upon us, eroding our very existence, changing us into empty versions of our former selves.

No one talks about that, do they? No one wants to acknowledge that men also suffer at the hands of abusers, no one recognizes that not all abusers are men, some of the most awful abusers are in fact women, men are subjected to the most awful of treatments and are expected to just get on with it.

The carry-on regardless attitude, what happened to the motto "its ok to not be ok?" or "broken crayons still color" all these cheesy sayings that are somehow meant to make everything better for you?

Saturday June 18, 2022, at 21.46hrs blocked your mother again as she was being so vile towards me and upsetting me and herself, after another whole day of constant messaging with her, trying to calm her down and reason with her, I was exhausted and just couldn't take anymore abuse from her.

Sunday June 19, 2022 at 13.12hrs I unblocked your mother thinking she would have calmed down overnight and she would be more reasonable in the morning the next day.

A picture came through to my phone of a fetal heart monitor machine, and a horrible message from your mother saying she was laying there listening to your heartbeat and how awful I am leaving her to do this alone, despite my offers of help that she has constantly rebuked and refused over the past 6 months, your mother saying how other couples are there together and she is sitting there all alone by herself, a position she has put herself in and blamed me for, I messaged back saying to let me know when she has another scan and that I will support her and go with her, her reply back was you are not welcome here, I will do this on my own fu@k off you cu@t.

Your mother went on saying what a cu@t I am for not supporting her, and then when I offer to support her, I am told to fu@k off and called a cu@t, I don't know what to do here.

Sunday June 19, 2022 at 13.46hrs I re-blocked your mother because the conversation took its usual nasty turn and your mother began abusing me again, this time I ended the conversation to attempt to prevent her from becoming abusive and hurting herself as well as me.

Wednesday June 22, 2022 @ 13.48hrs I unblocked your mother again hoping she had calmed down.

I needed some keys from your mother so I had to talk to her, it had taken me 6 months of trying to reason with her to get these keys, and she knew I needed them, the messages were short and to the point, surprisingly the conversation was more manageable, I arranged to get the keys back and the moment this had been arranged your mother immediately went off on her usual abusive rants towards me, she started accusing me of not trying to work things out, even though we couldn't due to your mothers violent abusive temper when things don't go her way, her delusional state of mind, her lying to herself and convincing herself that things were ok and that we never had a cross word between us the two years before I left.

There really was no reasoning with her madness so I just stopped trying, these circular conversations were ruining my mental health, I don't mind talking about things if I can see progress and we are starting to move things forward but that was not happening at all, your mother just kept going over the same things, she refused to accept my answers to anything, she wouldn't acknowledge that I also had feelings and that for the last two years my feelings has been totally trampled on and crushed, I knew your mother would never see things from my perspective so I stopped trying to put my side of the story across, I knew I was wasting my time and effort and anything I did say would be twisted against me anyway when she gossiped to her family and friends about me.

This is one of the reasons for me writing these letters to you, so that one day when you are old enough you can read this book for yourself and make you own mind up on what happened when you were so young, this is my way of getting my side of things over to you, this book also serves another purpose, one where I get to make a stand for the many other men who have also suffered in the same way as I have with your mother, I am not alone in my suffering and I know this.

Your mother told me to block her permanently as it was better for your mother, not for me at all, yet again, this all boiled down to how your mother was feeling and no one else, she told me that she couldn't cope being so upset all the time, even though this upset has always been caused by your mother and no one else, she sent messages saying she didn't want to admit to herself that things were over between us and that she loved me and was in denial of our relationship ending, the next load of messages I received from your mother finally admitted that I had been living in the spare room and that our relationship was over.

She accused me of not telling anyone about us being together for the two years we lived at the flat together, your mother said that I kept her a secret and didn't tell anyone I was with her because I was embarrassed by being with her, I hadn't kept your mother a secret, my family and friends knew perfectly well that we were together and that we were living together, but I am a private person and don't like talking about my issues, this book was really hard for me to write, but I have used writing this book as a way of coming to terms with the abuse that happened to me and as therapy to document it all and let it all go.

I didn't talk much about my relationship with your mother to other people, how could I tell people what was really going on behind closed doors? How could I tell people what was happening to me? I was embarrassed about your mother's behavior and the fact that I allowed the abuse to happen, I didn't really admit any of this to myself at the time so how could I freely talk about it to anyone else, plus your mother never allowed me to talk to other people without her being present so talking to other people was quite difficult.

It was only after receiving therapy that I was advised by my therapist to document everything and then let it all go, release it all so I could continue with my life having peace in my heart and calm in my head and between the therapists advice and my girlfriends' help documenting everything that this book was written.

After your mother admitting that we had issues, the next load of texts went back to being her usual demanding and threatening self, your mother started demanding I leave my girlfriend and go back to her, and that if I didn't leave my girlfriend that I would never see you, your mother said she would never allow me to see you after you were born.

Thursday June 23, 2022

The day started off with your mother messaging me saying that I chose another woman over her and you.

> *I didn't choose another woman over you*
> *Eliza, I left your mother not you.*

Your mother became abusive towards my girlfriend and started calling me and her awful names again, mainly the C word, all her messages were abusive, vile and nasty, your mother just never stopped being awful, this had become an every day accepted occourance now and your mothers' threats were losing their power as this had been ongoing now for months, I had grown tired of listening to your mothers shit.

Your mother then sent a photo of the entrance to the emergency room at Frimley Park Hospital from the back of an ambulance, your mother became even more abusive threatening me, saying she held me responsible if anything happened to you and I'm a cu@t.

After receiving vile abuse from your mother all day on Thursday June 23, 2022 at 17.07hrs I messaged your mother saying please don't message me ever again and I blocked her.

I'm sorry Eliza I just can't keep doing this.

My love always

Dad

CHAPTER THIRTY-TWO

The day you were born the painful truth.

June 24, 2022 – The day you arrived 3 months earlier than your due date, your due date was September 7, 2022 – you are now 1 day old.

Dear Eliza,

Unbeknown to me, today was the day you came into this world, and the day you were taken away from me. Your entry to the world was a traumatic one, an emergency birth due to medical conditions that needed immediate attention, Meconium Aspiration Syndrome.

What is meconium aspiration syndrome?

Meconium is the first feces, or stool, of the newborn. Meconium aspiration syndrome occurs when a newborn breathes a mixture of meconium and amniotic fluid into the lungs around the time of delivery. Meconium aspiration syndrome, a leading cause of severe illness and death in newborns, occurs in about 5 percent to 10 percent of births. It typically occurs when the fetus is stressed during labor, especially when the infant is past its due date, the reasons for causing such a condition all lie with the health of the mother, nothing to do with the father, but your mother blamed me for her gestational diabetes, even though she didn't follow a healthy diet, your mother blamed me for her unhealthy eating habits, and her lack of exercise, your mother blamed me for her high blood pressure, for her obesity, for her unwillingness to change her lifestyle for a more healthy one.

The truth is your mother blamed me for absolutely everything that ever went wrong in her life, my story is not just one solitary telling of events, my story is the same as many other men, who are pushed into silence within domestic abuse relationships, men that are terrified of speaking up for themselves in fear of reprisals from their female counter parts.

Your arrival in the world should have brought me happiness and joy but instead your mother but yet again this special occasion was robbed from me, because I had blocked your mother from June 23rd until unblocking her on June 28^{th,} I didn't know you had been born at all, and no one came to tell me either, I mean why would anyone come and tell me of our arrival, I am only your father what do I matter in all of this???

This was intentional, this was so your mother could exhibit power and control over me and my emotions yet again, forcing me to see that she held all control and that I was powerless.

Today was supposed to be a joyous occasion—the day you were born. Your mother has decided to keep you away from me, and I can't express how much that breaks my heart.

You are my daughter, and nothing will change that. I will always be here for you, even if I can't see you. I hope one day you'll understand the love I have for you, and maybe, you'll read these letters and know how much you mean to me.

With all my love,

Dad

CHAPTER THIRTY-THREE

*Tuesday June 28, 2022 – I unblocked your
mothers mobile hoping she had calmed down
enough to talk to – you are 4 days old.*

Dear Eliza,

Once I unblocked your mother, pictures of you were delivered to my phone, your mother had sent pictures to me, I asked what your name was and she told me it was Eliza, I got to see you in a picture for the first time and I was overwhelmed by it all, the stress your mother had put me through for the last 6 months I now hoped would end and that your mother would put your needs first, I wanted your mother to be civil so we could make arrangements for me to see you.

I wasn't allowed to feel this way for long, before your mother launched her attack on me, saying she felt humiliated and alone, and how I was to blame for everything, she told me all the partners of all the other mothers are in the hospital seeing their newborn babies in the premature unit and your mother was all alone by herself, again this could have been so different, but your mother was the one calling all the shots and making all the decisions, she intentionally pushed me out of everything and still held the control on whether or not I got to see you at all.

I messaged asking if your mother wanted me to come to the hospital to support you both and she immediately said no that I am not her partner and that your mother doesn't want me there because I am with someone else, but if I was to end that relationship then your mother would allow me to see you. She was using you as a weapon against me, saying I can't see you until I finish my relationship.

I spent the whole day messaging with your mother trying to arrange to come and see you, but your mother refused and would not allow me to come and see you at all. Your mother spent the whole day sending abusive hurtful messages then deleting what she had said, it got to 21.24hrs and I had just had enough of your mothers unreasonable messages and antagonizing behavior I told her that I was ending the conversation now as it was going in circles and upsetting for us both, your mother accused me of letting my girlfriend and my mother message your mother using my phone, which just wasn't true.

Wednesday June 29, 2022 – 5 days old.

Your mother started the day off with her usual insulting messages, I just didn't respond to anything she said all day. I wasn't going to allow myself to be pulled into her hurtful nonsense.

Thursday June 30, 2022 – 6 days old.

I messaged asking if your mother was home, she said she was not and asked why I had asked, I told your mother that I had bought you a little baby grow with born in 2022 written on the front in a premature baby size, a little soft bunny rabbit to put in your cot, a card and two boxes of your mothers favorite chocolates, I wrapped them all in wrapping paper and put them in a brightly colored present bag and dropped them over to your mothers flat.

At 12.39hrs I received the first message from your mother with an "x" on it for over a year, she wrote a message saying, "thank you for the presents x".

I thought that maybe your mother would be mellow now and start to be more reasonable about things regarding anything to do with you.

At 13.18hrs I asked to be put on your birth certificate and that triggered another rage episode from your mother saying that I don't deserve to be a father and that she will never put me on your birth certificate, your mother verbally abused me saying that I didn't deserve you and that I didn't deserve to be a father, again your mother had the control over this and I had to sit back and just accept it, your mother didn't want me on your birth certificate as it meant I would have parental rights, and your mother wanted all of the control over you.

I received a call from my mother saying there was a present bag left on her doorstep, it was the presents I had given to your mother for you, your mother in her anger had dropped the presents I had bought for you back to me and had put them on my mother's doorstep.

When I went over, I could see the little baby grow and soft bunny I bought for you along with the card all still inside, minus the chocolate I bought for your mother of course, she made sure she ate those!

Your mother became her usual abusive self, and we didn't speak with each other again until Tuesday July 5, 2022, when your mother was asking if I am moving my caravan from her horse yard. The conversations were strained and awkward and I was tired of trying to prevent your mother from attacking me, I was getting pretty fed up constantly treading on eggshells, trying to be civil and just receiving constant abuse and criticism no matter what I did.

I think I gave up trying to talk to your mother at this point and when your mother started messaging me again trying to guilt trip me into leaving my girlfriend saying I had made the wrong choices and that she hoped I was happy never seeing my daughter ever again and not getting to be a part of your life. I replied, saying I wanted to see you, but your mother was stopping me.

Your mother launched into yet another personal attack on me about how I don't deserve to be a father again and how I will never see you, another whole day of my phone receiving constant abusive messages from your mother, I stopped replying to her but she still kept sending message after message and after receiving 14 further messages and two awful messages that your mother deleted, she finally stopped.

Wednesday July 6, 2022 – 12 days old.

I saw you once in the hospital following your birth, I had been pleading and begging your mother to allow me to see you, after your mother realized that I was not going to finish my relationship with my girlfriend she finally said I could visit you and feed you at your feeding time, you had a tube inserted into your stomach and baby formula was slowly injected through this tube. It was lovely holding you and I sat just looking at you, you were so tiny and fragile looking and you were very light in my arms, once I had fed you your mother started asking me why I wouldn't leave my girlfriend and go back to live with her.

I think she allowed me to see you to attempt to isolate me and use my feelings for you to emotionally blackmail me into going back to her, when I said I didn't want to talk about that and that I just wanted to enjoy hold you your mother got angry with me again, and I had to leave.

I had only just left you when your mother started messaging me saying that she didn't want me to go to the hospital again, she felt too upset and she had told the nurses that I was a scum bag so it would ruin her story of being the victim in front of them, she told me that she would let me see you once you left hospital in about three weeks' time, I replied with the shortest answer of ok, as I really couldn't handle any further abuse from your mother as it was breaking me.

The next few days your mother kept sending and deleting abusive messages, I didn't reply, I just didn't have it in me to reply and I didn't want to start arguing again, I turned my phone on silent and I just left the phone on the side for the whole day.

Saturday July 9, 2022 – 15 days old.

Your mother sent a message saying, "how did it end up like this?" I didn't reply so she sent another message saying "I guess you don't care" I knew she was provoking a response out of me; I replied saying "I do care but I am not going to talk about it I'm done with arguing"

7 horrid messages sent by your mother that took all my self-control not to answer back to, then I asked how you were, trying

to divert the attention away from your mother's nasty temper.

Your mother sent a few photos of you, then launched into her usual emotional strike attack on me, a pattern I had identified after I had left her, it's called "hoovering" she goes softly to hook me back in, when I don't bite, she insults me or goads me, or she takes a pop at my manhood calling me childish or she attacks my character calling me weak and insecure.

I noticed that she was deflecting all the blame for her weaknesses and lack of character onto me, her insults were directed at me, but they were not actually about me, they were about how she felt about herself, I had started to research narcissistic personality disorder, and I was beginning to see real patterns in her behavior towards me and others close to her.

I remained strong and I didn't reply to any of your mothers messages, I was finally breaking her emotional hold she exercised over me, I was breaking free for the first time in years, and it felt good, I stopped acting on her insults and her threats, I started working on myself, and after your mother had sent 11 vile messages and 3 further deleted abusive messages she stopped sending them as I stopped replying to her.

The research I had read said stop replying when you are being victimized and abused, it stops everything, your mother used to goad me into reacting and defending myself with her false accusations of lying to her, so I would spend so much of my time trying to reason with her and defend myself, I could never get her to see things from my point of view, the advice said stop, so I stopped, and to my surprise it worked, not straight away, it did take your mother a bit of time to stop but in my eyes this was a good result for me, she stopped, I realized I had won my first victory here.

The next day – Monday July 11, 2022 – 17 days old.

Your mother messaged me asking where she could take your brother to jetski and I tried not to involve myself, I no longer wanted to be pulled in when it suited your mother and pushed out when I no longer served a purpose, I was trying so hard to break away from her and I knew this was another one of her ways to reel me back in by hooking me in with a question and trying to get me to arrange the details of it all.

I deflected the conversation onto you, you were my only concern now, and in my eyes you were the only connection I had with your mother, I didn't want to be involved with anything else to do with your mother at all, I asked how you were doing and when you were coming out of hospital, I also asked how much you weighed, your mothers reply was you needed to be 35 weeks old to leave hospital, in about three weeks and you currently weighed in at 3lb 2oz.

I asked again about being put on your birth certificate, your mother launched into a venomous rage attack sending and unsending vile abusive messages calling me all the names under the sun, I guess this will never happen, I want to be on your birth certificate, I want you to have me listed as your father, it is so you have your parents listed as your parents and assurance that if anything ever happens to either one of your parents that you are looked after and cared for as you deserve to be.

Your mother told me that she will never add me to your birth certificate because I am a cu@t. I give up I really do!

I'm at my whits end!

All my love

Dad

CHAPTER THIRTY-FOUR

Wednesday July 13, 2022, 19 days old.

Dear Eliza,

Your mother started the day off messaging me at 07.03hrs then deleted all the messages she had sent before I could read them.

I don't know whether I am coming or going anymore, I can't even progress one single thought from start to finish.

Your mother said it feels awkward talking to me normally with no arguing, she was finding it hard to accept that things had changed in my life, and because I didn't reply back to your mother straight away she accused me of having more important things to do and being with my girlfriend.

Your mother said that by me not replying to her straight away that she felt like I was busy doing fun things with my girlfriend and that I was saying you were not important enough to drop everything the moment your mother messaged me.

*This was just not true, you are important
to me and you always will be.*

Your mother said that when she messages me and talks about you Eliza that anything your mother has to say is important and that I must stop everything I am doing and listen to what she has to say immediately like an obedient dog!

When I tried to say that if I am at work, driving or riding on the track I can't just stop doing what I am doing at the very moment your mother messages and reply instantly, I tried to explain that she was being totally unreasonable and what she was asking me to do was damn near impossible, and that just led to me receiving more abuse from your mother, with threats of me never seeing you ever again unless I did exactly what your mother "told" me to do.

Your mother accused me of choosing my girlfriend over you and things just went from bad to worse, your mother sent a load of abusive messages then deleted them again, our whole relationship when we were together was forced choices made by your mother, she made everything a battle and forced me to choose her over what ever it was that I was doing at the time, she turned everything into this battle where she had to win, to prove to herself that by me choosing her that she is the best and very important, more important than anything else in my life.

It is ridiculous that she expects me to bow down to her every time she wants something, this goes way beyond a spoilt little child syndrome here.

Your mother has prevented me from seeing you or having any kind of access to you at all, then blames me for not coming to see you!!!!

> *That's like her sticking her head up her own*
> *arse and blaming me for the smell.*

My patience was tested to the max and was really starting to wear thin, I had been more than reasonable with your mother, and I had been more polite than maybe I should ever have been and yet all she did was continue to abuse me!!!

Thursday July 14, 2022 – 20 days old.

Your mother sent two pictures of you at 07.34hrs, then started sending and deleting abusive messages again.

I was being accused of not seeing you, I messaged back saying I wanted to come and see you but your mother wouldn't let me, your mother then sent vile messages saying I was seeing another woman and she didn't want me near you that you never know what you may catch off me, your mother was being insulting towards my girlfriend and had started to call her names too, I stopped replying to your mothers vile messages and at 11.43hrs she finally stopped messaging me and left me alone.

Friday July 15, 2022, at 07.21hrs – 21 days old.

I managed to send a message to your mother first for a change before she could start the day off on a negative note, I said I was done explaining myself and that I had had enough of her bullshit attitude of blaming me for everything and never taking any responsibility herself, I said that it didn't matter what I said or did, that I was always made out to be wrong and as such I had the right to walk away from her and any toxic situation she created that I didn't want to be included in.

I sent a message saying how your mother had changed all the scan dates and not told me the newly arranged dates, how she removed me from the birth plan, how she prevented me from seeing you in hospital, how your mother refused to put me on your birth certificate despite me asking several times, and how tired I had become with her using you as a weapon to control me, and still denying me access to see you.

I outlined the fact that I had pleaded with your mother over the last 7 months to stop being so difficult and to behave like an adult but that she was incapable of doing so, that I was totally fed up with battling with her on a daily basis and getting nowhere for it.

I said I was tired of being abused by your mother and I was done being reasonable, to which your mother replied calling me a joke and a selfish arsehole, I asked her to stop messaging me and I blocked her again.

Tuesday July 26, 2022 – I unblocked your mother – 32 days old.

There were messages that had been sent to my phone, abusive vile ones, that had been sent and immediately deleted again, so I couldn't read what your mother had said, I re-blocked your mother again, this was the only way I could ensure peace and protection from your mothers' abusive onslaught towards me.

When will this madness end?

All my love

Dad

CHAPTER THIRTY-FIVE

Application is in for the National
Association of Child Contact Centers

August 3rd, 2022 - A Visit to the
NACCC – 2 months old

Dear Eliza,

I applied to the National Association of Child Contact Centers (NACCC) to try to make arrangements to see you without involving your mother, this was the only option your mother had left open to me, and again the only way that would allow me to get to see you without your mother being present, Child Contact Centers are neutral places where children of separated families can enjoy contact with non-resident parents and sometimes other family members, in a comfortable and safe environment. Every year, this national organization, via its member centers, support families and children in their local community.

After considering how abusive your mother was towards me, this was the perfect way that I could establish and maintain a healthy safe connection with you as NACCC also delivers high quality training and support to ensure members of their staff are well equipped and knowledgeable to expertly handle these kinds of situations. In addition, there is a helpline which centers and parents can ring for advice and guidance, and a safeguarding helpline in the event of an issue arising at the center.

I felt that this was the best way to see you without your mother being present and without any drama and abuse being suffered by myself, so I made the application and paid a registration fee, I emailed your mother asking her to register on the site, she didn't need to do anything else, all she had to do was register, once she registered she would receive a reference number, and these reference numbers would be used to make all arrangements, there was no money for your mother to lay out either as I had taken care of all the costs involved, I paid for both myself and your mother, but your mother refused and told me to take her to court, she laughed at me while she belittled me yet again, there was no way your mother was going to agree to this method of me and you seeing each other because it conflicted with what she wanted, and by using the NACCCs method of access it meant that your mother would not be able to get me alone to herself so she could continue to abuse me and weaponize you against me further.

*So that was another way your mother used
to prevent me from seeing you Eliza and
I was running out of ideas here.*

Thursday August 4, 2022 – I unblocked your mother – 2 months old.

Your mother started messaging me saying she needed to talk to me and she tried to phone me but I had her blocked.

She said she was sick of other people getting involved in our business, even though these people she was speaking of she was the one who involved them in the first place.

Your mother got all abusive to me again and left me no choice but to block her again, this was becoming the usual pattern for us now, me blocking and unblocking your mother and her sending then deleting abusive messages.

Friday August 5, 2022 – I unblocked your mother – 2 months old.

Her messages started appearing immediately on my phone, asking me to come round to the flat to see you in person, your mother was saying how she had felt so stressed out being pregnant with you and was so angry at me that she had taken everything out on me and wanted to make it up to me.

Your mother said she wanted me to see you and be a part of your life, she wanted me to have regular contact with you but on your mother's terms and conditions not mine.

I finally thought things were moving in the right direction, that your mother had eventually accepted that we were no longer together and that is was important for me to be included in your life, she mentioned coming to see you 2/3 times a week every week.

I heard nothing more from your mother for a few hours until I received another message saying she needed to speak with me urgently, that she had something she needed to know right now, and that it couldn't wait.

I was at work when your mother sent this message as my phone was always on silent due to your mother constantly messaging it and she was giving me anxiety.

So I didn't see the messages until I arrived home.

Your mother left a voice clip saying she had wanted to know if I wanted to be added onto your birth certificate today and that the registrar was at the flat, I have never heard of any registrars visiting peoples personal addresses before, but hey, it could be a new thing, what do I know?

Your mother said that because she couldn't get an immediate answer from me she hadn't added me on your birth certificate, even though she knew I had been asking for 7 months to be added, she then sent a message saying I can be added to the birth certificate at any time in the future, but I know this isn't true, again another mind game of control which your mother knew damn well would upset me.

Your mother never had any intention of adding me onto your birth certificate, and I knew this, I stopped trying to make excuses for your mother behavior, I got wise and realized that everything your mother does is a cruel game of torture directed at me, that she carefully plots her revenge on me for leaving her, and she uses so many hateful games to hurt me.

*I'm not playing these games
anymore, I've had enough.*

All the while your mother gets to hold you in her arms, she gets to feed you and establish a close bond with all, but me, I get nothing with you, all I have are the few photos your mother sent to me of you when you were first born, all I can do is sit at home and wonder how you are, wonder what you are doing and what is going on in your life, I have no control over what is happening with you at all. What should have been a joyous occasion for me, a wonderful memorable event of having a child of my very own was again cruelly taken away from me by your mother's vindictive actions.

I knew she would never play fair, that she would have an argument and fight out of every situation she possibly could, and your birth was no different to anything else that had ever happened in our relationship with each other with another opportunity to use something that I cared deeply about against me yet again.

All my love

Dad

CHAPTER THIRTY-SIX

Saturday August 6, 2022 – Here we
go again - 2 months old.

Dear Eliza,

Your mother started messaging me, begging me to come and see you at the flat, all day she messaged me, begging me to go see you, she knew I would give in and go to see you, so I made a promise to your mother to come and see you tomorrow.

Sunday August 7, 2022 – I came to see you at your flat – 2 months old.

I was reluctant to visit you at the flat your mother lived in, as I knew that the moment your mother got me alone to herself she would abuse me, and I was correct in my thinking, I gave in to your mothers demands yet again, I came to see you at your home, and the moment I walked through the front door, it was slammed behind me and made me jump, I knew I was being held captive.

The atmosphere was dark and sinister, you could feel something was about to happen, I sat on the settee and had you on my lap when all hell broke loose, your mother started screaming and shouting at me, she started verbally attacking me, accusing me of doing and saying things that I had not done, your mother immediately shifted the blame for the breakup of our relationship firmly onto me, she totally ignored the fact that I had a mental break down caused by her continued abuse towards me, because this wasn't important to her at all, nothing to do with how I felt ever was important, it was always about your mother.

Your brother was in the flat too, he heard everything and naturally took your mother's side, he had been fed lies about me running off with another woman and abandoning you all, your mothers version of events were just not true.

I had left your mother due to her continued abusive nature, your mother had seriously affected my mental health, she had pushed me to a point where I could no longer survive in the toxic relationship I had with her.

I left your mother because she was abusive
and vile towards me, I never left you.

Your mother became so aggressive and abusive while I was there with you, it was starting to affect everyone in your flat, I was left with no other choice but to leave, this was to save your mother, you and your brother absorbing the upset of her screaming and shouting.

The moment I left, I received nasty messages from your brothers mobile, saying I was to blame for everything, that I just wanted to take you away and that I was having an affair before I left your mother, but that just wasn't true, he fiercely defended your mother, as a good son should, but he had been fed lies, and the whole situation had been a set up.

I had walked into yet another orchestrated vile toxic drama saga that your mother had specifically set up to make me look like the bad guy yet again, one of the very reasons why I left your mother in the first place, a toxic situation that I just could no longer cope with being mixed up in, the manipulation tactics very cleverly thought up to make me the bad guy in every single interaction with your mother, and it carried double weight by having witnesses present to tell her fable second hand to other people too.

I got the blame of course for upsetting your mother and making her cry, I was in a situation where I could never reason with your mother or tell my side of the story, your mothers drama sagas always outweighed anything I ever had to say. My feelings are never being considered, because in your mother's eyes I never mattered, only she matters.

I knew your mother had wound your brother up before I got there she had specifically worked him up to back her up and have a go at me for her too, your mother's tactics of manipulation and triangulation playing very important roles in making me out to be the bad person.

I had grown used to these repetitive behaviors, I had finally worked out your mothers patterns and how she used me to make her look like the victim, and I was not taking this kind of behavior anymore, I had learnt to use barriers, which infuriated your mother even further, because she realized she could no longer control me through her narcissistic twisted tactics, she held no power over me anymore, leading to her narcissistic violent rage outbursts getting even worse.

These triangulation dramas also played a massive part in the demise of my relationship with your mother, but she failed to realise this.

I blocked both your brother's mobile number and your mother's number too, so neither of them could message me.

This is never ending.

All my love

Dad

CHAPTER THIRTY-SEVEN

*August 14, 2022 - and so starts the emailing
from your mother - 2 months old*

Dear Eliza,

Because I have blocked your mother and your brother, she could not message me at all via mobile, and this infuriated her so much so that she resorted to emailing me instead.

She emailed today to say she had found the carpets for my caravan, first few emails were ok, then I received a massive email from your mother asking if being with my girlfriend was better for me, your mother said that if my girlfriend really loved me she would want me to come back to your mother and be a family, and here she goes trying to bend my mind to her will yet again, I didn't reply back to your mothers email, I knew she was trying to coerce me into doing what she wanted me to do, all she had done was change her approach, your mothers' tactic had gone from being loud, foul and abusive, to softer, more gentle and trying to use my emotions against me, but it was a tactic none the less, and one I was not going to fall for.

I didn't reply to the emails your mother sent after this.

August 15, 2022 – your mother took you over to my mother's house – 2 months old.

The next time I saw you was a few weeks later, this time at my mother's house, your mother had paid my mother a visit, and while you were there my mother called me to come over.

Your mother had asked my mother to call me over.

So, what did I do? Or course, I went over, I came running to see you after your mother had summoned me, your mother now on my territory in my mother's house, exerting her toxic dominance over us, spreading her toxic lies to my mother about how bad I am and how your mother is trying so hard to do the right thing for you Eliza, again using you as a weapon to cause mental and emotional pain on me and using my mother to do it too.

I knew that your mother had been contacting members of my family in secret behind my back, she thought I didn't know about it, but I did.

Your mother had previously approached my sister, messaging her trying to get my sister to see you without involving me, and when my sister didn't fall for this tactic your mother changed her plan and targeted my mother instead.

*My sister had ruined your mothers plan
of using her to get to me.*

My sister had replied back to your mother saying she will only see you when I had been allowed to see you and that what your mother was doing by using you to hurt me was wrong, that doing that causes mental harm on both me and you.

Your mother didn't like her plan being discovered and ruined, your mother was telling my family that I was refusing to see you, but in truth it was your mother refusing to let me see you.

*This was the most hurtful lie of all the
lies your mother told about me.*

*I tried so hard to see you, but I was
denied by your mother.*

Your mother didn't like being told no, the answer she received from my sister was not the answer she wanted at all, your mother wanted to showboat you off to everyone and anyone except for me, this was to punish me for leaving her (NOT YOU) and my sister's reply stopped her emotional blackmail games dead in their tracks.

But your mother wasn't going to stop there, oh no, she targeted my mother instead, knowing that my mother wasn't as strong as the rest of us, your mother anticipated my mother giving in to her because she desperately wanted to see you, what grandmother wouldn't want to see their grandchild? your mother banked on this, and my mother allowed your mother to enter her home, because my mother is not toxic, my mother is a lovely lady who has a heart of gold, and your mother had played on her emotions too, just like she had been doing with me also.

Once inside, she started snooping around at the photos of me and my new girlfriend that were displayed in photo frames on the fireplace, by the time I got to you at my mother's house, your mother was in a hateful rage.

The moment I walked into the front room where she was sitting with you, she started on me, and even with my niece and my mother both in the room too didn't stop your mother raising her voice at me, in my mother's house too, I couldn't escape from your mothers rage, it didn't matter where I went your mother found me and proceeded to abuse me.

Your mother at this point still didn't know the address I had moved to since my departure, it was for my own personal safety that I didn't want your mother to know my safe address, a place where I could rest and relax knowing she couldn't get to me and frighten me with her scary intimidation tactics she had used on me for years.

Again, I was left with no other choice but to leave my mother's house, while your mother got to stay and play the victim yet again, a scenario I had become accustomed to. I had learnt to accept the way your mother was and to just walk away and let her revel in her victories over me.

Your mother had conditioned me to
accept her abuse over time.

121

I never saw you again after this day.

As I write this, I am overwhelmed with a mix of emotions. There is sadness for the moments we will never share, and also for the moments we have already missed out on, but there is also immense love and gratitude for the brief time that I did get to see you and hold you.

I am ever hopeful that your mother will eventually calm down enough to allow me to see you.

All my love

Dad

CHAPTER THIRTY-EIGHT

All Hell Broke Lose

August 17, 2022 - another email from
your mother – 2 months old

Dear Eliza,

I got another email from your mother saying if I didn't leave my fiancé that I would never see you ever again, I didn't reply.

August 21, 2022 – today is the day your mother
discovered that I had gotten engaged – 2 months old

I received another email from your mother with pictures of my fiancé and her children contained in the body of the email, your mother was vile and abusive accusing me of seeing a woman older than me with older children, your mother upon discovering the identity of my fiancé had removed her pictures off her social media and had sent them to me abusing me and insulting my fiancé.

After discovering my fiancé identity and stalking her online, your mother had discovered that we had got engaged, your mother had taken screen shots of this news and sent this to me in the email too.

Your mother also used my fiancé pictures to create numerous dating accounts and sex accounts using my fiancés pictures and mobile number and my fiancé started to receive abusive phone calls from withheld numbers and messages from strange men asking to meet up with her, this went on for the next few years.

Really not funny at all.

I just cannot believe the depths that your mother will stoop to, just to cause a scene and make trouble, I'm totally shocked by her behavior.

August 24, 2022 – your mother emailed me accusing my fiancé of phoning your mother and abusing her – 2 months old

Your mother emailed me saying my fiancé was calling her and being abusive over the phone, and the email your mother had sent to me said that any time I wanted to leave my relationship with my fiancé and repair the relationship with your mother and you then I could let her know.

Your mother ended her email by threatening by saying she was going to the police.

This was the final straw for me.

I had been subjected to so much abuse from your mother, I had suffered abuse from the time we were living together, I had been abused all year from January right up until now in August and now your mother was also targeting my fiancé too, I reached the point where I had taken enough from your mother and I just wanted her to stop abusing me and leave me the hell alone.

We saved your mother the trouble of going to the police, we involved the police ourselves, we could see what your mother was doing, she was trying to create a drama saga and accuse my fiancé of abusing her when my fiancé wasn't at all.

We decided to put a stop to your mothers' antics straight away, this had been going on now for long enough and it just had to stop, your mother had to stop, and if she wasn't going to stop by herself then we were hoping the police would stop her for us!

I knew your mother would cause trouble for me if I ever left her, she always said she would ruin my life.

I knew that she would cause trouble for any other woman I started dating after her too, and once she discovered the identity of my fiancé, I just knew your mother would target her and abuse her too, and over the next few years your mother tried everything she could to discredit my fiancé and make her look bad, just like your mother had done to me for years by gossiping about me and bad mouthing me behind my back to my family and friends.

The police were of the opinion that your mother was either sending these messages of hate to herself or getting one of her friends to do it for her to make my fiancé look bad.

I always knew that no matter who I dated after your mother that we would be in for abuse, but I really wasn't expecting all the things your mother did to my fiancé over the next few years.

The police came round, they looked through all the abusive text messages your mother had sent to me all year since January, and I was able to show the police even more messages dating back even further to June 2020 from your mother.

I was advised that this was not acceptable behavior from one person to another no matter what the circumstances were, the police were quite alarmed at the things your mother had been saying, and they were now concerned for my safety and the safety of my fiancé too.

I showed the police all the emails I had been receiving from your mother after I had blocked her mobile phone and your brothers, the police informed me that finding another way to make contact with a person after being blocked was considered harassment and it s prosecutable offence.

The police advised me to email your mother a "cease and desist" email outlining the fact that any contact received after we had sent this email would be considered to be harassment, and classed as a criminal offence.

I sent this cease and desist email in the presence of the police, and to my surprise your mother instantly replied while the police were still with us, they read the reply your mother had sent, which was foul and abusive and we were advised by the police advised us not to reply.

We were told that we had to be the ones who maintained silence here as your mother was just incapable of doing what was right, the police mentioned something about your mother having antisocial tendencies and they had seen this kind of behavior many times in their careers before and if we adhered to their advice that eventually your mother would stop.

The police told me to stop making myself available for your mother to abuse so easily, then they went on to inform us of ways to protect our personal safety, they advised us on installing CCTV at our home, and cameras that record on our vehicles, the police checked our locks on our front door before leaving too and advised us to contact a lock smith to perform a safety check on our home, and to make sure that all windows and doors were closed and locked at all times.

I was now feeling even more apprehensive now, more so than I ever had

before, but there's really no telling what your mother is capable of doing.

All my love

Dad

CHAPTER THIRTY-NINE

And so it begins

*September 4th, 2022 – your mother dropped
the leisure battery for my caravan to my
mothers' house – 3 months old*

Dear Eliza,

Your mother emailed me again today, as I still had her blocked saying she was going to drop the leisure battery for my caravan at my mother's house, your mother knew I was away for the weekend with my fiancé as she had her flying monkeys reporting our very move directly back to her, like Queen Bee, your mother had been told that we had posted on our social media and showed a picture of us on a beach in Wales.

I read your mother's email, but on the advice of the police I did not reply.

My mother rang me later on in the day to say a battery had been dropped on her doorstep, I told my mother that your mother had dropped it and that we would be home the following day.

*How on earth did the brakes on my fiancé
car get tampered with and fail?*

September 5th 2022 – how on earth did the brakes on my fiancé car get tampered with and fail? – 3 months old

Coincidentally, the weekend that we were away on the day that your mother dropped the leisure battery to my mother's house, the brakes on my fiancé car were tampered with and subsequently failed while she was driving to work on the motorway!

This was reported to the police and recorded as criminal damage this was truly scary as it was considered as "attempted murder" but "whoever" did it, made damn sure there were no witnesses!

September 6th 2022 – your mother emailed me AGAIN saying my fiancé was abusing her – 3 months old

I received an email from your mother accusing my fiancé of sending a text message with a picture of your mother calling her fat, I didn't reply back to your mothers email, and when I didn't reply back, an hour later I received yet another email from your mother with a different picture supposedly having been sent to your mothers mobile phone, your mother was accusing my fiancé of texting your mother again calling her fat and ugly, I didn't reply back to this email either.

I received a third email from your mother saying "I swear if your fiancé messages again I'm going to the police" then your mother wrote "please tell her to stop" then she ended her email by saying that "my fiancé had just cost me seeing you Eliza and that your mother will NEVER let me see you"

YOUR MOTHER NEVER HAD ANY INTENTION OF EVER LETTING ME SEE YOU – EVER

Your mother enjoys using you in her mind games to hurt me way too much!

I never replied to any of your mothers emails, I just reported it to the police under the reference number we had been given, I told the police that ever since you were a three week old fetus in the womb your mother has been threatening that I will never see you, my fiancé never influenced me not being able to see you at all, your mother never had any intentions of allowing me to see you, it's the ONLY control she had left over me and she had been using you as a weapon against me ever since she found out your existed.

*Absolutely shameful behavior from a mother of a
child, what kind of mother weaponizes a child?*

Not only is your mother punishing me, but she is also punishing you Eliza, by keeping me away from you, you grow up without the presence of a father in your life, I think your mother is doing this to you out of jealousy and spitefulness, all because your mother didn't have a father figure in her life when she was growing up, so she made sure that neither you nor your brother had a father figure in your lives either, so she can keep all the pain and hurt inside of her going, dragging forward all that septic toxic vileness and feelings of loneliness and emptiness and putting it all into you too, its unforgivable in my eyes.

All through the rest of September my fiancé continued to receive silent phone calls to her mobile, she had fake friend requests being sent to her social media accounts and lots of people asking her strange questions about her life, she knew that your mother was behind all of this, so she just deleted, blocked and ignored them all.

Now your mother knew the identity of my fiancé your mother and her friend had started to target my fiancé with abusive messages of hatred and jealousy, relentlessly ringing her mobile day and night, your mother was sending abusive messages and your mothers friend was sending vile abusive voice clips, yet another triangulation drama saga engineered by your mother and her vile enablers, your mother had told her friend to target my fiancé and to abuse her.

The abuse I received from your mother and her friends was horrendous, and now my fiancé was being targeted too, so we approached the police. The police could see how aggressive and abusive your mother was, so they advised me to apply for a Non-Molestation Order with the powers of arrest.

So that's exactly what I did.

Bollocks to your mother, I've reached the end of my rope with her, she deserves the book being thrown at her for all the hurt she is causing other people.

All my love

Dad

CHAPTER FORTY

My heart hurts so badly why is your
mother doing all of this?

October 16, 2022 at 19.45 hrs – I received an abusive
call from one of your mothers' friends – 4 months old

Dear Eliza,

We placed a picture of you in the living room, so you would always be with us, but your mother saw this on our social media and demanded that we take it down, your mother got one of her friends to phone us, message us and leave vile abusive voice messages on our mobiles calling us names and abusing us saying our relationship was sick, fuc@ked up and twisted, I had never known such hatred before in my life.

Your mother was not able to contact me as I had her and your brothers' mobiles still blocked, so she told her friend to abuse us on her behalf instead, she was still hellbent on saying the hateful things she wanted to say, and nothing was going to stop her saying them either, even blocking her didn't stop her.

Even after we sent an email to say stop contacting us, but your mother is not one to be "told" what to do, in your mothers' eyes she tells everyone else what to do, not the other way round, so because she couldn't contact me, she got her friend to do it for her!!!!

Your mother's friend was vile and awful, swearing at me and calling me names, she sent me four long winded messages calling my fiancé nasty names and calling me names too, when I stopped replying to her messages she started sending recorded voice clips to my phone too, these were just as vile.

I received one recorded voice clip, then another, then another, she was just pressing record and babbling on and on, she was driving in her car with her kids too, how unsafe was that?

When I played back the voice clips you could hear her vile common voice spitting out her words of hatred and venom, I could hear your mothers' words spewing from her filthy mouth, the messages were awful, I blocked this friend of your mothers to stop her contacting me anymore.

My sister was so angry at me being constantly attacked that she messaged your mothers friend telling her to leave me alone and that it was none of her business at all, my sister asked why this friend of your mothers was making it her business to get involved in something that had nothing to do with her, all my sister got back was more vile abuse, so my sister blocked her.

We were left with no choice but to remove all photos we had of you and throw them in the bin, I wasn't even permitted to have photos of you in my own home, your mother had total control over everything to do with you, I wasn't allowed to attend your scans, my name wasn't added to your birth certificate, I was and still am denied seeing you in person and now your mother is demanding that the photos of you that she had sent to me herself were to be removed from display in my home and destroyed.

This broke me into a million pieces.

October 18, 2022 – my fiancé messaged both your mother and her friend – 4 months old

My fiancé messaged both your mother and her friend at the same time, my fiancé said this had been ongoing for way too long now, there was no need to involve other people in what is going on and she appealed to both of them to stop abusing us. My fiancé asked for both your mother and her friend to stop paying so much attention to stalking and harassing her and get on with their own lives in peace.

My fiancé asked your mother to be considerate of other people's feelings here and to stop focusing solely on her own selfish needs, there was no swearing in my fiancé messages to both your mother and her friend, she was polite and considerate considering all we were receiving was non-stop abuse, once my fiancé had sent this message she immediately blocked your mothers phone, but before she could block your mothers friends phone, she had received replies back from your mothers friend.

They were two ausive and rude voice clips, my fiancé thanked your mothers friends for her abusive response then immediately blocked her.

*This is behavior from two grown women
in charge of young children!*

October 18, 2022 – the great blocking party started – 4 months old

After we received such abuse from your mothers' friend, both me and my fiancé proceeded to block all your mothers' family and her friends on all social media platforms, we blocked all their mobile numbers they were all using to contact us with too.

We had specifically asked your mother not to contact me and now she and her family and friends were targeting myself, my fiancé and my family, this had to stop.

My family also did the same.

*This was like trying to deal with a bunch of 5 year old
children throwing temper tantrums in a sweet shop!*

All my love

Dad

CHAPTER FORTY-ONE

Its starting to look a lot like a
monkeys' tea party now

October 27, 2022 – For crying out loud
please stop woman – 4 months old

Dear Eliza,

I started to receive withheld number calls on my mobile when I was at work, I knew this would be your mother because she would just not accept being silenced in this way, when she had something to say she JUST HAD TO SAY IT and she was not giving up trying to contact me.

I stood firm and did not cave in and answer the phone though, you'd be proud of me if you knew what strength was needed to stop myself giving into your mother.

October 31, 2022 – so the terror begins – 4 months old

I came out to go to work today and the tires on van had been let down, there was no punctures so "someone" had let them down intentionally,.

Wow! I wonder who that could have been??

November 01, 2022 – the drive bys – 5 months old

I saw your mother driving past my house today when I was leaving to go to work at 07.30hrs! What a coincidence hey?

My fiancé phone has been ringing all week with withheld number calls, she never answered any of them, she just ignores them and lets the calls go to answer.

I am getting so many withheld number calls too, but like my

fiancé I don't answer any of them, I know it is your mother, I can just feel it.

November 15, 2022 – Withheld number nuisance calls – 5 months old

I was getting so many withheld number calls today I gave in and answered one of them and surprise surprise, guess who it was?

Yep! Your mother!

I hung up immediately the moment she spoke, and I knew it was her, but she rang back again straight away, I didn't answer, she rang back several more times before she stopped calling my phone.

Because I didn't answer my phone to your mother, she emailed me saying she didn't want to argue she wanted to talk to me sensibly, your mother wrote in her email that we used to be friends why can't we just talk normally, but I wasn't the one who couldn't talk normally that was your mother!!

I had gone home for lunch on this day and I told my fiancé that your mother had tried to call me and was now emailing me too, my fiancé said maybe your mother was trying to say she was sorry and that she had finally come to realize that the only way forward in all of this is to talk to each other civilly like mature adults, we both sat there thinking your mother had finally come to her senses and this was her way of reaching out to me.

I emailed back saying I would answer the phone if she called it, I also said that I didn't want to argue anymore and if your mother became abusive that I would hand up the phone and not talk to her again.

Your mother called me again, I answered the phone to her, my fiancé was sitting right next to me and could see I was shaking as I answered the phone to your mother, but the moment I did answer, your mother immediately launched into a verbal attack on me yet again accusing me of being an arsehole and a cu@t.

Both myself and my fiancé were in total disbelief, your mother hadn't come to her senses at all, she had been festering about not being able to contact me directly, it had annoyed her that I had taken the control on her not being able to contact me and the moment she was able to talk to me she abused me, so I put the phone down on her, your mother lied AGAIN, when will I ever learn that she is incapable of telling the truth?? I felt so stupid.

My fiancé said it wasn't my fault, that the blame for how your mother reacts is entirely on her, that she needed to take responsibility for her own behavior and stop blaming other people all the time, I could see she was right but I still felt stupid for trusting your mother and believing her lies, you'd think I would have learnt by now wouldn't you?

Putting the phone down on you mother just angered her even more, and she began ringing my phone to try to get me to answer it, but I wouldn't, she kept ringing back again and again, but I would not answer her, and because I wouldn't answer her, she emailed me AGAIN.

Your mother sent three emails that
I didn't reply back to.

She was abusive and defensive saying she was trying to talk to me, and I wouldn't listen to her, she called me rude for not listening to her and ended her last email by saying that I was asking for no contact so she will fuc@ing give it to me and to fu@k off, she told me her whole family had me blocked and that she will make sure no one ever talks to me again!!

Another lie of your mothers!

Looking back now I think your mother made contact with me, just so she could make herself feel like she had instigated the no contact rule between us, she couldn't accept me telling her that I no longer wanted to speak to her at all and that I wanted to maintain a strict no contact rule, so she had begged me to talk to her, just so she could scream at me that "She wanted to go no contact with me" this sounds so insane when you read it back! But it's true, your mother could never accept that I wanted nothing more to do with her at all, her behaviour is childish!

> *I don't know what mental mind games your mother is playing but I really don't want to be a part of them anymore, I'm so done!*

November 29, 2022 – here starts the online stalking and gaining of intel – 5 months old

People are stalking my fiancé online, they are trying to snoop on her profiles and social media accounts, my fiancé has upped her security on all her accounts, she has changed all her passwords and implanted multi factor authentication on everything, she has received so many hack attempts this month she has lost count. My fiancé removed all her profile pictures from all accounts as your mother and her friend have been signing her up for dating profiles and sex sites using her photos. Childish behavior, I have no words for any of this I really don't.

November 30, 2022 – Jingle Bells, Jingle Bells – 5 months old

The day before our court hearing all our outside Christmas decorations have been vandalized, we have an idea who this is, but without witnesses the police have informed us that there is nothing they can do.

I swear, if I even see your mother anywhere near my Christmas decorations that she will be visiting the accident and emergency ward of the local hospital to have my Christmas robin removed from her arse!

What possible pleasure is she gaining here by kicking over decorations outside our house? and who is looking after you while your mother is driving over to our house causing criminal damage?

I really hope you don't grow up to be a giant arse like this Eliza.

All my love

Dad

CHAPTER FORTY-TWO

What can I possibly do here

December 01, 2022 Court Hearing at Slough
Family Courts for a Non-Molestation Order
on your mother - 6 months old.

Dear Eliza,

I received a court date of 1st December 2022. The judge listened to what I had to say but your mother denied everything, even though evidence of her abuse along with three A4 folders of supporting witness statements was delivered to the courts 7 days prior to our hearing date.

The judge was very lenient on your mother, but seeing as she deflected the blame onto me, saying I was the one harassing and abusing her, we both had the Non-Molestation Order applied upon us, I felt this was extremely unfair and totally unjustified seeing as I was the one who applied for the order and paid for it too.

There were strict instructions that neither party was to contact the other party, in person, directly or indirectly, by email, phone calls or messages for a year until the order ended on 1st December 2023 the following year.

The judge also ruled that I was to be allowed to see you, your mother named a third person that all correspondence between me and them had to go through to make all access arrangements regarding my visits to see you, your mother was also ordered to perform a DNA test to prove I was your father as there were doubts to whether or not I was.

I came away from this hearing very disappointed that the judge hadn't taken my claims of harassment and abuse suffered at your mothers hands seriously enough, but I was hopeful that now things would change and that your mother would have enough time to calm down and speak to me respectfully once the order was lifted in a years time.

December 4, 2022 – Letter received from the Child Support Agency (CSA) – 6 months old

On December 4th 2022 I received a letter from the Child Support Agency (CSA) saying your mother had made a claim against me financially as I was your father, I phoned the agency and spoke with a service operative, who informed me that if I didn't think I was your father I was within my rights to request a DNA test to be performed, of which I would initially pay the costs, but if it was found upon performing the test that you were not my child and I was not your father, then your mother would have to pay the costs, I explained to the operative that your mother had banned me from the scans, removed me from all involvement with you before you were born, and refused to put my name on your birth certificate following your birth, I explained to the lady that I had NEVER denied your existence and that I was trying to attempt to arrange suitable access to see you through your mother who was making the whole situation more difficult than it needed to be.

I informed the lady of me paying to register with the NACCC and your mother refusing to register too and allow me to have access to see you through the contact centers, I also explained to the lady that there were rumors circulating regarding the parentage of you and that I may not be your father at all, seeing as the rumors being spread foretold of a time that your mother kicked me out of the house for a weekend so she could hold a party at her flat, and this happened to coincide with the exact date that you were conceived combined with the people who had attended that party were talking about the wild things that were going on that night that didn't include me, as I was staying with my friends after your mother threw me out just added to the rumors that you may not be mine.

So, I requested a DNA test, the lady told me she would get back in touch with a date for me to attend a medical Center of the CSAs choosing, and that your mother and you would have to attend on the same day too, but at different times to save us meeting up with each other.

December 6, 2022 – Oh really??????? Maybe there is some truth in the rumors then after all? – 6 months old

I received another letter from the CSA saying your mother had dropped the claim and was unwilling to perform a DNA test.

What woman refuses to perform a DNA test on a child that she is adamant that I am the father of?

A woman who is not sure of the fatherhood of her child perhaps?

The abuse we received leading up to Christmas that year continued, and your mother failed to adhere to the court order with both her and her friend continuing to harass and abuse both me and my fiancé.

Your mother also broke her promise to the courts to make arrangements for me to see you and she never had a DNA test done either, your mother had no intention of adhering to the court order at all, she blatantly laughed at the judge all the way through the hearing with this smug smile on her face.

I have been to court, pleaded my case, but the legal system is full of holes, and it feels like I'm fighting a losing battle.

All my love

Dad

CHAPTER FORTY-THREE

Christmas, the time to be with family

*December 25, 2022 Your First
Christmas – 6 months old.*

Dear Eliza,

Merry Christmas Eliza today is a day filled with mixed emotions.
It's your first Christmas, and I should be there with you, sharing in
the joy and wonder of the season. Instead, I am here, writing to
you, trying to bridge the distance that keeps us apart.

I hung a special ornament on the tree for you, a little angel with
your name on it. As I decorated the tree, I imagined you here with
me, your eyes lighting up at the sight of the twinkling lights and
colorful decorations my fiancé has decorated our house with so
many decorations that it looks like Sants Grotto and I just know
that you would love it here, I imagined us opening presents with
you here with us, then going over to my see my parents and
taking you with us, my parents would have loved to have seen
you on Christmas day.

Christmas is a time for family, and it's hard not being able to be
with you. I hope that one day you will be with me at Christmas
time, but until then, know that you are my shining star, my
precious Eliza. Merry Christmas, my love.

All my love

Dad

CHAPTER FORTY-FOUR

New Year heading in

January 1, 2023 - Happy New Year – 7 months old.

Dear Eliza,

Happy New Year, my little girl. As the clock struck midnight, I made a promise to myself this year, my resolution is to stay strong and hopeful, no matter how difficult things may get.

The start of a new year is a time for fresh beginnings and new hopes. I want to believe that this year will bring us closer together, that somehow, I will find a way to be with you and your mother will calm down enough to be able to talk civilly to me.

I think about all the milestones that lie ahead—your first steps, your first words, your first birthday. I want to be there for all of it. I want to be the father you deserve, to show you the love and support that every child should have.

So, here's to a new year, Eliza. A year filled with hope, love, and the determination to be with you. You are in my thoughts always, and I will never stop thinking of you.

January 10, 2023 – this madness is just not stopping – 7 months old

Your mother has continued to harass both me and my fiancé all over the Christmas period and into the New Year, and she was arrested under caution in January 2023 and held on bail conditions until April 2023 while the police carried out further investigations.

Upon your mothers discharge from the police station in January she immediately deactivated all her social media accounts and mobile telephone numbers she had been using to stalk, harass and abuse both me and my fiancé, she rewrote old posts on her accounts so it looked like she was innocent and that I was making things up about what her and her friend were doing to me and my fiancé. A clever tactic your mother has always used in her methods to stalk and harass others in the past.

Your mother started using disposable mobiles and throw away sims, she created lots of fake accounts in random peoples' names, this meant she could continue to stalk, harass and abuse both me and my fiancé without anything being traced back to her all the time she was under police bail conditions.

Very clever. Touche

The police informed us that your mother was released from bail conditions in April 2023 as they could not gain any firm evidence of her harassing us online because she had deactivated her old accounts in her name and the police said no new activity was showing on any of her accounts, well of course not, she made new fake ones in different names!

It's been a whole year since I left your mother and she is still abusing me and I am still suffering mentally at her hands, plus I am still not seeing you.

I wonder what you are doing now and how much you have grown. I see other children your age and compare your development to theirs and I am hoping that one day we will sit together and talk about all of this madness and compare what happened to both of us, so we can unravel the hurt caused by your mother.

All my love

Dad

CHAPTER FORTY-FIVE

I got married and you weren't there to see it

June 14, 2023 – I got married today – 12 months old

Dear Eliza,

I got married today, I really wanted you to be one of my flower girls along with my niece, but that would never happen as your mother would never allow it, we had to keep the details of our wedding a secret because we knew your mother was desperately trying to find out where we were getting married, knowing your mother she would have gone out of her way to spoil our day, so we never announced any times, dates or venues until after our special day.

Yet another happy time in my life that had to be suppressed because of your mother, I knew she would cause trouble for us, so we had to make sure nothing was posted about visits to wedding shops, or any details about who was making our cake or anything, we had to plan our wedding like a covert military operation, we were denied all the excitement of the build-up leading to our big day for fear of your mother discovering any details.

We only posted pictures on our social media the day after our wedding!

Your mother's insecurity and jealousy ruins everything, and even though we are no longer together she is still ruining everything she can for me.

I knew your mother would make things difficult for me but I had no idea she would be this spiteful and nasty towards me.

All my love

Dad

June 24, 2023 - A Special Day, I missed your First Birthday – 12 months old.

Dear Eliza,

Happy first birthday, the day that should have been filled with joy and celebration, I found myself heartbroken and helpless knowing your mother is driven by spite and bitterness, I missed the chance to be a part of your special day with you in person.

I celebrated your birthday with my wife instead, we were in Scotland on our honeymoon we went out to dinner in a Scottish restaurant in the Highlands to celebrate on your behalf, we bought you a card and wrote in it, we know your mother will never allow us to give you this card so we brought it back home with us and we now keep it safe at our house along with all your other birthday and Christmas cards, we keep buying them hoping that one day you will be able to come and visit us and see for yourself that you were thought about and truly cared for in our household.

and that you are being deceived by the worst kind of lies about us and that your mother is the one responsible for us not having the father daughter relationship that we should have been having right from your first day of being born.

Missing these precious moments lost in time that you and I will never be able to get back. Every day I am kept away from you is another day of torture and pain inflicted upon us both, we both suffer because of your mother's anger! What a selfish woman. Keeping us apart like she does had nothing to do with your nor me, your mother is not thinking about the pain she is inflicting on your Eliza, she is driven by her own selfish need to punish me for leaving her, but all she will do by acting like this is hurt you more.

I'm so sorry Eliza

All my love

Dad

CHAPTER FORTY-SIX

*Our second Christmas without
seeing each other.*

*December 25, 2023 The Power of Love, your second
Christmas without me seeing you – 18 months old.*

Dear Eliza,

Christmas is here, this is your second Christmas, and I have not seen you now for 17 months.

You are now 1 and a half years old, you must be walking and talking and I wonder what you look like and how your little voice sounds, I find myself missing you more than ever this year. The holidays are a time for families to get together and share stories from the past and hopes for the future.

I wonder at your personality, are you fun loving, are you a happy little girl?

We put up ornaments on our tree with your name on them again this year, we had a little white polar bear and a small elf, these are to remind us that you are a missing part of our lives and that you may not be here with us in person, but you are always in our hearts, and until I know for sure whether I am your father or not, then I will continue to love you with all my heart until that day.

My wife has bought you a little Christmas present and she wrapped it up and put it under the tree, she looked at me and said "you just never know what tomorrow may bring" she smiled at me and continued putting presents under the tree.

My wife has been buying birthday and Christmas presents since you were born, she has wrapped them all and put them under the bed in the spare room, she seems to think that one day you will come looking for me, that you will have so many questions about why I wasn't around when you were born and why I was not involved in your upbringing.

My wife has organized folders of the messages between your mother and me, you can read for yourself how hard I tried to get to see you and how your mother blocked me at every opportunity she could, my wife says that by documenting everything this way that it would show you a true account of events and that you could see the facts being presented to you in an organized way, with the information being easy to see what was really said and you would be able to dismiss any non truths that you had been told while growing up.

My wife also said that you would be able to make your own mind up about the events that led to my leaving your mother, and that after reading through everything that I would not really need to explain myself to anyone anymore, she also said that it would not be fair to attempt to influence you in any way at all, and that I had to allow you to asborb the information at your own pace and ask your own questions in your own way too, I do agree with my wife.

My wife said that these folders are my way of releasing the trauma that your mother put me and you through, so until that day when you come looking for your answers these folders are safe with me and will be held for you to read when you are ready.

We have also written four books now telling our side of events that happened, from leaving your mother, to my fiancé being stalked and harassed for years by your mother and her family and friends, and now my book especially for you, if I didn't care for you would I write a book for you? How many fathers can say they wrote a book for their children when they separated from their exes?

We both felt that it would make you happy to discover that we had been buying you presents all your life, all the time we were not in contact with you, but still thought of you, my wife said it was a lovely thing to do, my wife has a great outlook on life, she has compassion for people and true empathy, something your mother totally lacks.

CHAPTER FORTY-SEVEN

Curiosity is killing the cat

*June 24, 2024 - Your Second
Birthday – 24 months old.*

Dear Eliza,

Happy second birthday, my little girl. Another year has passed, and I find myself missing you more than ever. It's hard not being able to see you, to watch you grow, to celebrate these special moments with you.

We baked a cake for you, we decorated it with flowers and your favorite colors, and as we lit the candle, we made the same wish —that one day, we will be together, that I will get to hold you and tell you how much I love you.

I spent the day thinking about you, imagining what you might look like now, what new things you have learned. I hope you are happy and healthy, that you are surrounded by love and joy. You deserve all the happiness in the world.

You are always in my heart, and I will never stop loving you. Happy birthday Eliza.

All my love

Dad

September 1, 2024 A Father's Determination – 27 months old.

Dear Eliza,

Today marks another milestone that I am missing—your first day of preschool. I imagined you with a little backpack, excited and a bit nervous about this new adventure.

It's hard not being able to be there with you, to see your smile, to hold your hand and walk you to your classroom, I am seeing all my friends posting up pictures of all their little ones that are starting preschool today.

But even though I cannot be there physically, I am with you in spirit. I think about you every day, I wish that I were a part of your life.

You deserve to have a father who loves you, who supports you, who is there for you. And I want to be that father to you, Eliza. I want to see you grow, to share in your achievements, to be there for your struggles and your triumphs.

I love you more than words can say.

All my love

Dad

November 1, 2024 My wife wrote a letter to your grandmother – 29 months old

Dear Eliza,

My wife wrote a letter to your grandmother today and posted it through her door, my wife is tired of the continued harassment she is receiving from your mother and her family and friends, she caught your mother out yet again using a profile she had made in your grandmother's name to stalk and harass her at work.

Your mother has been stalking and harassing my wife online now since June 2022, the month you were born, this has been ongoing now for 29 months, the whole time you have been here.

In this letter my wife tried to appeal to your grandmother to see reason and talk to your mother to try to persuade her to stop acting so childishly and be reasonable, my wife has appealed to your grandmother to meet face to face to attempt to resolve the ongoing harassment we are receiving from your mother.

My wife outlined all the cruel things your mother and her friends are doing to my wife, and she wants it all to stop, my wife has said that this silliness has been going on for way too long now and it needs to stop.

Your mother is a difficult person and there is no reasoning with her, I have come to accept that now, it's one of the many reasons I left your mother in the first place, your mother is just not capable of holding adult conversations regarding adult issues, and she is not capable of being reasonable full stop.

My wife also appealed to your grandmother to speak with your mother and try to get her to make contact with me to resolve our issues and make arrangements for me to start seeing you, but knowing your mother I really don't hold out much hope of her ever allowing me to see you, she will keep us apart for as long as she possibly can, that way it ensures the maximum amount of damage she can inflict upon us both.

November 7, 2024 – Well that answers that then doesn't it? – 29 months old

It was just six days after delivering this letter that my wife had her email address that she had given to your grandmother spammed, six days!

Less than a week after delivering the letter to your grandmother, a woman that we asked for help in reasoning with your mother!

I suppose this is my answer, isn't it? Your grandmother, like your brother, is siding with your mother, I expected it as blood is thicker than water.

All my love

Dad

CHAPTER FORTY-EIGHT

November 12, 2024 Your mothers birthday –
and my final letter to you - 29 months old

My Final Letter to you!

Dear Eliza,

I have now accepted that I am never going to see you again, this weighs very heavy on my heart, I am hoping that one day this book finds you and you read it and know that you are loved by me, that I fought for you as hard as I could, but in the end I had to stop, your mother didn't add me onto your birth certificate so in England that means I have no rights at all, I have no rights over what happens to you, I have no say in what happens in your life, I don't get to be involved in any decisions made on your upbringing nor your welfare, I don't get to choose the best schools for you, I don't get to attend any of your life events nor any of your special occasions, I have been forced out of your life totally by your mother.

Your mother knew that by not adding my name to your birth certificate that I could not fight to have access to you without forcing a DNA test, of which your mother has refused twice, once ordered by the courts back in December 2022 and also by the CSA in December 2022.

I don't get to watch you grow up, I miss everything from your first steps, cutting your first teeth, your first words, which I am hoping was "dadda" just to piss your mother off!

I don't get to help you learn to ride your first bike and I don't get to take you out for play time in the park. I have accepted I will never push you on a swing or spin the roundabout to make you giggle uncontrollably and I have accepted that I will never get to comfort you when you are upset, hurting or just need a cuddle.

I will never bathe you and put you in fresh smelling clean clothes, we will never sit on the settee and snuggle up to watch your favorite movie together while you fall asleep in my arms, I will never get to put you to bed at night and kiss you softly on your forehead before you fall asleep.

Your mother gets to hold you while I get to watch strangers raising their children, there are many situations today where the parents have separated for whatever reasons, not all children have both parents at home, some children are lucky enough to have two mothers and two fathers where a relationship has broken down and their father and mother met new partners and moved on with their lives, but these people put the welfare of their children as the top priority and they are all mature enough to co-parent together, still providing the love and the support that their child needs, and ensuring that their child does not suffer due to their breakup and indifferences.

These types of parents work hard to make sure their child and other children they had together are not made to suffer because their parents no longer live together, but that is not what happened in our case, you have one parent who was nasty and vindictive who punished the other parent and forced them into leaving a very toxic abusive relationship that would never have worked out for the better and then played the victim, blaming me for everything that was wrong in our relationship, this kind of behavior is childish and immature and I have been targeted by your mother in the most hurtful of ways imaginable, both you and me have been made to suffer unnecessarily.

We are both being punished for your mothers selfishness, we both miss out on being together and forming an unbreakable bond between us, we will never have any kind of bond together, your mother has made sure of that, and I have to sit and wait years for you to be old enough to come looking for me, to ask if I am your father, and in all honesty Eliza I can't tell you whether or not I am or am your father, we would have to do a DNA test first, if it came back that I am indeed your father all the lost years we will never be able to claim back, they will be lost forever, and all the times we could have been having fun together and going on adventures will be missed forever.

I don't get to be a part of your life journey and that is the price I paid for daring to leave your mother.

The mental damage enforced on us both in unrepairable, you growing up without your father and me growing older without my daughter, both of us being intentionally kept apart because your mother cannot find it in her heart to allow us to be together, just like she did with your brother and his father too, your mother poisoned your brother against his father and stopped him from seeing his father for years, all the while she destroyed any chance of the two of them forming any bonds together, your mother did this because your brother's father had an affair behind your mother's back, something I never did but always accused of doing and punished for. I was punished for the sins of your brother's father!!

But then again, looking at how your mother has lied about me, the story she told me about your brothers father may also be untrue, I will never know, and neither will you, the truth will be buried under years of lies, buried so deep that we have no hope of the truth ever surfacing, another reason why I wanted to document everything now while it is all still fresh in my mind, to ensure that the facts don't get lost over time.

I know that by the time you able to come and see me that you will have formed your own opinions of hatred towards me from all the lies that you will have been fed by your mother and her family and friends over the years, and that your idea of me being a bad person will be so firmly planted inside your head that it will be impossible for you to shake off and accept any other opinion of me other than the ones that were formed for you by other people.

I also know that no matter how hard I will have to work to try and prove to you that you have been lied to about me your whole life would be in vain and that you would still think bad of me.

I am not the monster your mother will be making me out to be, far from it, but you will have been made to feel nothing but hatred towards me for so long that neither of us would be able to put any of the hatred aside and start a newfound happy relationship between us.

But I will always live in hope that one day both you and me will find all the answers we are both searching for, a day in the future where we both get to find out if I am truly your father or not, until the day you come to find me, I wish you every luck and love in the whole world and I wish the best of everything for you, I hope you get all the things you wish for and have the happy life you so deserve, I cannot undo the hurt that has been caused and I cannot force your mother to see reason and to do the right thing, that is her decision and hers alone, I have no control over what your mother does.

I never did have any influence or control over anything your mother did, I have tried my hardest to try to reason with your mother but I am not able to, I admitted defeat a long time ago and made some hard decisions to move on with my life for the safety of my mental health. The whole toxic situation was unhealthy and was showing no signs of ever improving, your mother will NEVER see it this way.

Even though I have been accused of being self-centered and selfish this is not the case, I grew weary trying to convince your mother otherwise, she is set in her thinking and will not be moved at all, I sit here waiting for you to become educated and to be able to make your own mind up about things, I want you to find your own answers for yourself and ask your own questions in your own way, I know this will only happen over time, and that is all I have right now.... Time!

I know you will be angry at me for not fighting harder for you, but what else can I do but walk away and wait for the day you come to me instead.

All the way through all of this I have NEVER had the choice, I have never had the control and I will never have the control where you are concerned, I hope that one day you take the control over yourself and make the best decisions, I want the best for you, I want you to succeed in life and most of all I want you to be happy.

This is my last letter to you Eliza until we meet face to face one day in the future,

All my love

Dad

CHAPTER FORTY-NINE

*The effects of being intentionally
separated from you*

The Weight Of Absence

The absence of your presence is a constant weight on my heart. Every day without you feels incomplete, as if a part of me is missing. This void can be overwhelming, leading to feelings of sadness, anxiety, and even depression. The nights are the hardest, lying awake, wondering what you are doing, if you're happy, if you miss me too. The silence can be deafening, and the longing for you becomes a physical ache.

Coping Mechanisms

To cope with this, I have tried to find ways to channel my emotions positively. Writing these letters to you has been a significant outlet, a way to keep you close even when we are apart. I have also turned to exercise, meditation, and therapy to help manage my emotions. Talking to a therapist has provided me with tools to navigate this challenging time, helping me understand that it is okay to feel vulnerable, to grieve the time we are missing.

The Stigma Of Mental Health

There is often a stigma associated with mental health struggles, especially for men. Society sometimes expects us to be strong and stoic, but I have learned that true strength lies in acknowledging our vulnerabilities. I want you to know that it is okay to seek help, to talk about your feelings, and to prioritize your mental health. It is a lesson I wish I had learned earlier, but I am grateful for the support I have found now.

The Importance Of Hope

Despite the challenges, hope has been my guiding light. The hope of seeing you, of holding you, of being a part of your life keeps me going. It is this hope that motivates me to keep fighting, to keep pushing through the darkness. Every small victory, like getting a new lawyer or hearing positive news from the court, reignites that hope and strengthens my resolve.

The Impact Of Isolation

Isolation is another significant factor. Not being able to share the joys and challenges of parenthood with you leaves me feeling isolated. There is a sense of loneliness that comes with not being able to be there for you, to support you, to watch you grow. This isolation can amplify feelings of despair and hopelessness but knowing that I am not alone in this struggle helps. Connecting with other parents who are going through similar situations has been a source of comfort and solidarity.

Building Resilience

Through this journey, I have learned a lot about resilience. Each setback has taught me to get back up, to keep moving forward. Resilience does not mean that I do not feel pain or sadness; it means that despite these feelings, I find the strength to continue. It is a lesson I hope to pass on to you, that no matter how tough things get, we have the capacity to endure and to find a way through.

A Promise To You

Eliza, my love for you is a powerful force that keeps me going. Even when the days are dark, and the weight feels unbearable, my love for you gives me strength. I promise to continue fighting for you, to be the best version of myself for you. I want to be a father you can be proud of, someone who never gave up, no matter how hard things got.

A Better Tomorrow

I believe in a better tomorrow, a future where we can be together, where we can make up for lost time. This belief is what sustains me, what helps me get through the toughest days. I dream of the day when I can tell you all of this in person, when we can look back on these letters and see how far we have come.

Final Thoughts

Writing these letters has been therapeutic, a way to process my emotions and share a part of myself with you. I want you to know that it is okay to struggle, to feel overwhelmed, and to seek help. You are never alone, and I will always be here for you, loving you, supporting you, and fighting for you when I am allowed to be in your life.

You are my heart, my soul, and everything, Eliza. I love you more than words can say, and I will continue to hold onto the hope of a brighter future for us.

Until one day in the future when I hope we will come face to face with one another.

CHAPTER FIFTY

Conclusion

As I bring this book to a close, my heart remains full of hope and love for you, Eliza. These letters, written in moments of longing and love, are a testament to the unbreakable bond I have always felt for you, despite the distance and the barriers that have kept us apart.

The journey has been fraught with challenges, heartaches, and the insurmountable obstacles created by a vindictive ex-girlfriend's lies and hate campaign. But through it all, my love for you has never wavered. It has remained a constant, a beacon guiding me through the darkest of times.

My dream of seeing you, of holding you, and of building a strong father-daughter relationship remains as vibrant and powerful as ever. I believe in the resilience of love, in its ability to heal and bridge even the widest of gaps. I believe that one day, we will be together, and we will build a relationship grounded in truth, love, and understanding.

To you, Eliza, I say this: Never doubt that you are loved. Never doubt that I have fought for you and will continue to do so. The lies and hate that have kept us apart can never diminish the truth of my love for you. You are my heart, my soul, and everything.

One day, when we are finally together, we will have the opportunity to create new memories, to share the joys of life, and to support each other through its challenges. We will have the chance to write new chapters in our story, chapters filled with love, laughter, and the deep bond that we were always meant to share, but sadly robbed of.

Until that day comes, these letters will stand as a testament to my enduring love and hope. They are a piece of my heart, a way for you to know me and understand the depth of my feelings for you. I hope that when you read them, you will feel my love and know that I have always been with you in spirit, even when I could not be there in person.

The future holds the promise of new beginnings, of healing, and of a relationship built on the foundation of love and truth. I look forward to that day with all my heart and soul. Until then, know that you are loved beyond measure and that my hope for our reunion will never fade.

With all my love, forever and always,

Dad

A MESSAGE TO FATHERS IN THE SHADOWS

Dear Fellow Fathers,

If you are reading this, you too are living through the agony of being separated from your children. The pain of not seeing your child is a unique and profound sorrow, one that leaves a mark on your soul. This chapter is dedicated to you, to acknowledge your struggle, to offer solidarity, and to share some wisdom from my own journey.

The Depth Of The Struggle

Being denied the chance to see your child following a toxic breakup is one of the most heart-wrenching experiences a father can face. The longing to be there, to witness their milestones, and to share in their joys and sorrows can consume you. You may feel isolated, overwhelmed by the injustice, and crushed by the weight of your emotions. These feelings are valid, and it's important to acknowledge them.

Finding Support

In times of such intense pain, finding support is crucial. Reach out to friends, family, or support groups for fathers in similar situations. Talking to others who understand your pain can provide immense relief and solidarity. They can offer advice, share their own stories, and remind you that you are not alone.

Legal Advice And Advocacy

Navigating the legal system can be daunting, but it is essential. Seek legal advice from professionals who specialize in family law. Understand your rights and the legal avenues available to you. Organizations that advocate fathers' rights can also be invaluable, providing resources and support to help you fight for your right to be a part of your child's life.

Self-Care And Mental Health

Your mental health is paramount. The stress and emotional toll of being separated from your child can lead to depression, anxiety, and a host of other issues. It is important to take care of yourself, even when it feels impossible. Engage in activities that bring you peace and joy, whether it is exercise, meditation, hobbies, or spending time with loved ones. Seeking professional help from a therapist can also provide you with tools to cope with your emotions and build resilience.

Staying Connected

Although you may be physically separated from your child, find ways to stay connected. Write letters, keep a journal, or record messages for them. Share your thoughts, experiences, and love in these tangible forms. These can be a source of comfort for you now and a precious gift for your child in the future, showing them that you never stopped thinking about them.

Holding Onto Hope

Hope can be a lifeline. Despite the challenges and setbacks, hold onto the hope that one day you will be reunited with your child. Focus on the long-term goal of building a relationship with them, even if the path to get there is fraught with obstacles. Your love for them is a powerful force, and it can sustain you through the darkest times.

Being The Best Version Of Yourself

Use this time to work on becoming the best version of yourself. Whether it is through personal development, education, or career advancement, channel your energy into positive growth. This not only helps you cope with the pain but also prepares you to be the best father you can be when the time comes.

Advocacy And Change

Consider becoming an advocate for change. Share your story, raise awareness, and support initiatives that seek to reform family law and protect fathers' rights. Your voice can contribute to a larger movement aimed at ensuring that no father has to endure what you are going through.

FINAL THOUGHTS

Remember, you are not alone in this struggle. There are countless fathers who share your pain and are fighting the same battle. Draw strength from this collective experience and know that your love for your child is a powerful, unbreakable bond. Keep fighting, keep hoping, and never stop believing that one day you will be reunited with your child.

With solidarity and hope,

A Fellow Father in the Shadows

ABOUT THE AUTHOR

Kimberley Alice is an author known for her compelling explorations of toxic relationships, especially focusing on men's experiences with narcissistic women.

Her debut book, *Six Years a Friendship and a Baby*, delves into the complexities of friendships that turn into relationships and end after being impacted by narcissism.

In her second book, *Me and My Shadow*, she shares a personal account of being stalked and harassed online by her husband's ex-girlfriend, shedding light on the emotional toll and the reality of cyberstalking.

Kimberley Alice continues to explore these themes in *Shadows of Betrayal*, which tells the story of a couple enduring similar harassment.

Her latest book, *Letters to Eliza*, is a poignant narrative of a separated father's attempts to connect with his daughter through letters after being alienated by a narcissistic ex-girlfriend. Kimberley's work provides insight into the struggles and resilience of individuals affected by toxic relationships and aims to foster understanding and awareness of a growing issue in todays world.

www.ingramcontent.com/pod-product-compliance
Lightning Source LLC
Chambersburg PA
CBHW072142090426
42739CB00013B/3260